The Monstering of Myra Hindley

Nina Wilde

Foreword by Judith Jones and Beatrix Campbell

WATERSIDE PRESS

The Monstering of Myra Hindley
Nina Wilde

ISBN 978-1-909976-34-4 (Paperback)
ISBN 978-1-910979-12-9 (Epub ebook)
ISBN 978-1-910979-13-6 (Adobe ebook)

Main UK distributor Gardners Books, 1 Whittle Drive, Eastbourne, East Sussex, BN23 6QH. Tel: +44 (0)1323 521777; sales@gardners.com; www.gardners.com

North American distribution Ingram Book Company, One Ingram Blvd, La Vergne, TN 37086, USA. Tel: (+1) 615 793 5000; inquiry@ingramcontent.com

Cataloguing-In-Publication Data A catalogue record for this book can be obtained from the British Library.

Printed by Lightning Source.

e-book *The Monstering of Myra Hindley* is available as an ebook and also to subscribers of Myilibrary, Dawsonera, ebrary, and Ebscohost.

Published 2016 by
Waterside Press
Sherfield Gables
Sherfield-on-Loddon
Hook, Hampshire
United Kingdom RG27 0JG

Telephone +44(0)1256 882250
E-mail enquiries@watersidepress.co.uk
Online catalogue WatersidePress.co.uk

Table of Contents

About the author

Criminologist Nina Wilde was born in Holland and first met Myra Hindley in Cookham Wood Prison, Kent in 1993, where she was engaged in research. She was shocked when the Governor told her that Hindley had already been in prison for almost 30 years, thinking that because sentences of this length are unknown in much of Europe there must have been some kind of mistake. Then she discovered the power of the media which was also at various times directed at Nina once her close friendship with Hindley became public.

Acknowledgements

Some of those people I need to thank did not wish to be mentioned by name but they know who they are and my appreciation is due to them. I would particularly like to thank Judith Jones and Beatrix Campbell for agreeing to write a Foreword; Dr Gwen Adshead for her kind contribution below; and Peter Kirker for kind permission to use his letter (*Chapter 4*).

I approached forensic psychiatrist Gwen Adshead and explained to her the project I was working on. I asked her if she would be willing to contribute to it with her views. Based on a late draft of the manuscript I sent her, she replied to me, and described my work as, "A very sad story of how fear and hatred allows injustice to flourish." She continued:

> "Your book demonstrates how Ms Hindley was treated in a qualitatively different way from other people who have committed similar offences against children, and others like her convicted under joint enterprise; it also offers a perspective on how politics influences the exercise of law. It also raises the issue of how and whether people change over time; and whether anyone can be said to be the same person after 34 years of life, however lived.
>
> I'm not sure I can say anything much about how [Myra] came to involve herself; and how/why she felt unable to break away. As you say, she was a young woman living at a time and in a culture when women did what they were told and men were expected to be masters and were always right. If I knew more about her upbringing I might speculate about her attachment style; children exposed to violence in the home are at risk of developing an insecure attachment style, which affects later attachments to partners. She describes an intense attachment to Brady as well as a fear of him; and this is a common picture that we see in women who have helped or failed

to prevent a man hurting others. But whether it explains anything is much harder to say; in fact I am not sure that anything could explain her failure to act. I think you are describing a real existential issue; namely that you met a different person to the person who was involved with Ian Brady all those years ago; a person who had been profoundly changed by her experience. She wasn't able to say much about what happened; and so I'm not sure that others can, or should. In my experience it is for the offender to tell their story, and as she said it may be a horror story that (unlike the movies) does not have a neat or satisfying ending.

For what it's worth, I think she became a national scapegoat for that part of the social mind that is cruel and has contempt for vulnerability."

I would also like to thank Bryan Gibson, of Waterside Press, for enabling the book to see the light of day, having said that although he may not agree with every line of what I have written it thoroughly deserved to be published, especially as it will be available in libraries and on the internet for a very long time. Even if it meets with resistance now, it may be quite different when people come to look back on how one case above all others came to symbolise attitudes to penal affairs, how one prisoner was singled out for special treatment, even into the 21st century.

Nina Wilde

September 2016

To my mother for her unfailing help and support.

To the memory of my friend Anne McArthur, without whose inspiration and occasional own "input" this book could not have been written.

"There is no greater tyranny than that which is perpetrated under the shield of the law and in the name of justice"

De Montesquieu, *Spirit of the Laws*, 1748.

"'I'd love to help you but . . . I've got a family, responsibilities, other things to consider and so forth.' There was always a reason not to help; probably it was more a question of being too afraid. And I hope that the deafening silence around Myra's case from the various liberal-minded justice and human rights groups and also women's groups stemmed indeed from fear to speak out rather than wholesale tacit approval of how her case was dealt with and of her treatment."

Chapter 10

Foreword

We were schoolchildren when the Moors Murders splashed in black and white on Granada reports and the front page of the *Manchester Evening News*. And so it began, the cultural—and we now realise political appropriation—of Myra Hindley and Ian Brady as the worst of humanity, locked-up. Our betters promised that we were kept safe, physically and morally, from these people until either they or we died, whichever came first.

In 1999 we collaborated with the great late theatre director Annie Castledine to draw on our long professional experience in the field of violence against women and children, to discover whether themes which, we had already discovered, were largely untellable in the news media, could perhaps be tolerated in the theatre.

Over several workshops we learned that poetry and even beauty released in drama could support an audience and a creative team to "tell the untellable." We created Gail, a researched but ultimately imagined character, who had made a conscious decision to kill a child, but who had been convicted of a lesser charge. She had never disclosed the truth. She had her reasons. We decided that the questions which needed to be asked of this character could only be asked by someone who knew about and indeed had been imprisoned for killing children.

Why not go for the "worst," we asked ourselves. And so it was that we undertook detailed research into Myra Hindley for the play, which opened at West Yorkshire Playhouse in 2002.[1] A revised production opened at the New End Theatre, Hampstead in January 2003. It was

1. *And All the Children Cried.*

critically acclaimed, won *Time Out* Critics' Choice and was produced again in 2004 at Battersea Arts Centre.

Our character was called Myra, not Hindley. We wanted to make it clear that though researched, indeed relying heavily on her own published words, she was our creation and her purpose in the play was to service our investigation of Gail. We were rescued by her death from the ethical dilemma: should we approach her, should we show her the script?

We hold to the view, however, that this would not have improved our "created" character. In a sense, then, "Myra" was always invented. Before the play opened some parts of the mass media, often seeking assistance from Mrs Winnie Johnson, a bereaved parent, questioned whether we should dramatise a character based on Myra Hindley. Our answer was that our aim was to explore in dramatic form issues which are difficult to represent in other—or in any—forms.

We spoke with Winnie Johnson. It was a calm and thorough discussion, for which we were enormously grateful. We were powerfully affected by her dreadful pain and loss, and her dignified determination that Keith should not be forgotten or overshadowed by the debates about Hindley and Brady.

The play and the after-show discussions confirmed our feeling that there is a hunger for discussions about why people, especially women, are taken to such cruel and desperate extremes, about how justice is and should be administered whilst honouring the victims, and, of course, the part played by institutional and cultural misogyny in our judgement of women. This hunger is often abbreviated in populist discourse: "How could they? Hanging is too good for them." But we think this traduces a larger curiosity. Ironically, misogyny had allowed Gail to seemingly "get away with it" and, of course, in our play, to leave Myra with no chance of rehabilitation at all. No one—having seen the play—said it was a project that was not worth doing.

Nina Wilde is writing into this political tumult. She has a particular and unique perspective. She has a professional interest in justice, the penal system and rehabilitation. And she has had a personal relationship with someone, who, she argues strongly, would never have been a candidate for either justice or rehabilitation, irrespective of her own personal journey. She has tried something brave and complicated. Quite rightly this book tracks the political and cultural tangle about Hindley as if it were ungendered, as if it were uncluttered by age and class. We would suggest that perceptions of women in the criminal justice system are always misogynistic unless they're not.

Myra Hindley appeared to us to be so recognisable as a clever, but unschooled person (as Myra described herself in our play); a working-class girl with a brain, living with domestic violence and physical abuse. Misogyny erased the scalding impact of domestic violence: and physical abuse in her childhood that, we would suggest, took away her judgement, her potential, and her moral compass.

Paradoxically, prison was the only environment in which Hindley could engage with other people, and they with her, as someone other than, or someone who was not only Brady's woman, the Moors murderer—a person who (to paraphrase Helen Prejean, the campaigner against capital punishment) was more than the worst thing she had done in her life. Prison was where her relationship with Nina Wilde flourished and faded, not least because the criminal justice system required nothing more of Hindley than "good behaviour." Prison certainly does not require an offender to face her history.

Nina Wilde offers a comprehensive exposure of the lack of logic, the sexism, and politicians' fear of the tabloids in the making of legal and political decisions. She shows, too, through the prism of Hindley's prison experience, how we squander what we might learn about violence, from a population that is uniquely shaped as both victim and perpetrator.

Judith Jones and Beatrix Campbell, October 2016

The authors of the Foreword

Judith Jones trained as a social worker and has worked throughout her career in the field of mental health, violence against women and children, and child protection. She began to write drama in 1999 with her partner Beatrix Campbell.

Beatrix Campbell OBE is a prizewinning writer and broadcaster, and over many years has been a Writer in Residence in various prisons.

Introduction

Perhaps few people would expect a sympathetic treatment of one of the UK's most notorious serial killers. But questions which demand to be asked include: "Why do the media need to create demons?" and "What impact does this have with politicians and others?" Exactly 50 years after Ian Brady and Myra Hindley were sentenced to life imprisonment for the Moors Murders of 1963–65 and approaching 15 years since Myra's death in prison, after one of the longest sentences in Britain served by a woman, this book is my attempt to raise what I believe are some quite legitimate questions about what I also think are quite serious issues.

My personal connection with Myra

I was a very close friend to Myra who I first knew when I worked in prison and then visited in various prisons over many years. So I will try through that relationship to provide some fresh insights concerning one of the most talked-about and possibly most vilified women in Britain. I invite readers to try and understand her like I did, to hold back the worst of their prejudices and fears as I try to show how the media singled out Hindley as a monster, a symbol of all that is deviant in women, and the politics at play around her captivity, that caused a succession of career-led Home Secretaries to treat her as a special case.

I also compare by way of example how things are done in some other European countries and outline how the UK itself routinely releases others equally bad (or possibly far worse) quietly and away from the public gaze, including for equally political (if opposite) reasons.

Predictably my book is one to which some people may well react with dismay, but that is the whole point. Though we may wish not to be reminded of bad things and might not like to admit it, are we not, once the rights and interests of the victims have been acknowledged, talking about injustice and a mob mentality, something that panders to base instincts and infects our approach to law and justice overall?

It has been said that in the past half-century few if any girls have been called Myra and others have changed their name, a measure of just how deep-seated the phenomenon, of the creation by the media and others, of a hate figure became.[1] After moving to London and meeting new friends there, it did happen on occasion that when I mentioned my connection with Myra I suddenly didn't hear from these friends anymore. All kinds of tactics were used to preserve her negative image. Those who did try to help her, and there were a good few what I like to think of as decent people, were frequently vilified by their detractors or labelled as misguided do-gooders or woolly-minded liberals. They became part of the problem and were often subject to adverse criticism and bad-mouthing.

As I explain in *Chapter 10* the phrase, "I'd like to help you but..." became a recurring and resounding indicator of how any known association with Myra made individuals, support groups and organizations look to excuses. They too, it seems, were caught-up in what passed for "public opinion," or may have risked losing funding.

Structure of the book

In *Chapter 1*, I explain how I first met Myra, quite by chance, at Cookham Wood Prison and look at some of the background to her case and the experiences of women prisoners in general. *Chapter 2, The Outsider* explains how I came to English prisons as a foreigner so that my whole perspective was different, uncluttered by the received wisdom about this dreadful woman, and how I found it strange that someone had already been incarcerated for what was then 30 years and with no prospect of release. I also say something about two cases from other jurisdictions.

1. "I think it is a pretty name, although it has become obsolete in the UK because of the murderer Myra Hindley, I have a very beautiful friend who was christened Myra, but in later life changed her name to Eve because of all the nasty comments she received!": see http://www.babynameshub.com/girl-names/Myra.html

Chapter 3 looks at how long-term imprisonment affected Myra, as it would anyone, and what I call 'the nature of her injustice'.

Chapter 4 looks at what with hindsight stands out as the shameful media coverage and politicking around her, the 'monstering' of the title of this book. I explain how the verb "to monster" was apparently coined by tabloid feature writers to describe their tactic of degrading people in the pursuit of "news." So the title of the book is quite deliberately in the active tense to show that the demonising and vilification of Myra was no accident or subconscious gesture but a campaign fuelled by a variety of people, interests and concerns of the kind that obtain comfort, or in some cases derive benefit, financial or otherwise, from the discomfort of or malign effect it has on others. It eats into our minds, disfigures our reason and eventually becomes part of a game in which the winner is the one who can come up with the deepest cut or "keep the pot boiling". So discomfort may be far too gentle a word.

Chapter 5 and *6* return to the subject of Myra's reputation and the role of a media and press driven by the need to ensure profits at all cost. In *Chapter 7* I look at *Myra as Public Property* whilst *Chapter 8* shows how the never very clearly articulated case against her release was enlivened *ad infinitum* in later years together with some of her experiences at that time, how she learned to anticipate and recite official responses to her applications by rote and in unison as they were read out to her by prison governors. *Chapter 9* looks at her offer to undergo hypnosis and what I term "other distractions" which were used by politicians and others, so that as public property the totem that Myra Hindley had become was never allowed to disappear from public view.

Finally, as I have already indicated *Chapter 10* looks at some of the spurious reasons put forward by those who maybe should have taken a bolder approach to their true feelings, who really wanted to help but could not bring themselves to do so publically or put their name to it.

Realising how hard it is for readers to keep track of events across such a long timespan as Myra's own life and her life imprisonment I have included a *Timeline* immediately following this introduction.

Some words of encouragement

Being always on the defensive can wear you down. Not knowing what readers might think of my work but fearing the worst and before submitting it to a publisher, I showed it to a number of people including a retired senior Home Office official, a former member of David Ramsbotham's (now Lord Ramsbotham) team when the latter was HM Chief Inspector of Prisons. This was the official's personal and kind response:

> "Above all the script reads as a personal journal charting your special relationship with Myra. It is almost certainly unique from that perspective. The highlight for me is Myra's beautiful letter to you which is so revealing. She loved you because you were real to her. You fetched her some normality from the reaches of the world outside, where people were perceived to be free. By the time you came into her life she was a very different person from the woman who first entered prison, and it is easy to imagine the sheer delight she must have felt on realising that you were someone she could talk to as a very close and trusted friend. By the time you met her she had long since forgotten what being free in the mind really meant. If as you say she had experienced physical and emotional abuse during her upbringing, and as we know later had come under the grossly disordered influence of Ian Brady, she may not have connected with anyone in her life in the way that she appears to have done with you."

Indeed, I hope that the way in which Myra "connected" means that I can contribute something fresh and constructive to what remains, even after all this time, a sensitive and contentious debate about how we treat prisoners who are locked away for extensive periods of time. How we distinguish the truly dangerous from those who have been rehabilitated, and what part, if at all, notoriety should play in all of this. It is also interesting to note this Home Office official's comment about the influence of Ian Brady, something that I try to draw out in the book and to show how once this had weakened with the passing of the years—I would say to vanishing point—how Myra's pre-existing normality appears to have returned (or as he astutely observes, "some normality," given the context).

When we criticise others for their lack of normality, or what they may have become or may have done, we should also look to our own good fortune in avoiding the circumstances that led them to it. As Myra once said (see *Chapter 6*), "I also believe I'm hated not just because I'm feared, but because people fear that they could have been me." Of all the things we have invented her to be, to my mind, the most important one is that she is "not us." This reminds me of the following quote by Aleksandr Solzhenitsyn:

> "If only there were evil people somewhere insidiously committing evil deeds, and it were necessary only to separate them from the rest of us and destroy them. But the line dividing good and evil cuts through the heart of every human being. And who is willing to destroy a piece of his own heart?"

I hope that what follows is a balanced account, or as balanced as the circumstances permit when arguing against the grain of what is perceived to be public opinion. My publisher thought an alternative title for the book could well have been "I Would Like to Help you But…" I felt "A Story of Obsession" would also have been apt, as this element appeared to have been pretty persistent in Myra's life.

Timeline

1942	Myra Hindley, born 23-7
1947	Primary school
1953	Secondary modern
1961	Starts work at Millwards, meets Ian Brady (born 2-1-1938). He a stock clerk, she his typist. He was 23, she 18
Victims:	
1963—12 July	Pauline Reade, 16 years and five months
	Myra writes letter to her friend May, that in the event anything happening to her, May was to tell the police that Brady was responsible
1963—23 November	John Kilbride, 12 years and six months (the day before John F Kennedy had been assassinated)
1964—16 June	Keith Bennett, 12 years and four days
1964—26 December	Lesley Ann Downey, ten years and four months
1965—6 October	Edward Evans, 17 years and nine months
1965—7 October	Ian Brady arrested
1965—11 October	Myra charged as accessory, with 'harbouring Brady knowing he had killed John Kilbride'

1965—12 October	Police digs on the moors begin
1965—November	Suspension of Capital Punishment (abolished 1969)
1966—19 April to 6 May	Trial at Chester Assizes. Ian Brady found guilty of all three murders, Myra Hindley guilty of Evans and Downey murders, not guilty but an accessory in the murder of Kilbride
1966—May	Myra starts her sentence in Holloway Prison
1966—October	David Cameron born and Theresa May celebrates her tenth birthday
1968	Myra meets Lord Longford
1969	Moon landing
1969	Rupert Murdoch buys *The Sun*
1972	Governor of Holloway Prison takes Myra for a walk on Hampstead Heath
1974	Trial at the Old Bailey for attempted escape plot from Holloway Prison, with Patricia Cairns (prison officer) and Maxine Croft (inmate)
1976	Myra wins Koestler Award
1976	Attacked in Holloway Prison
1977	Transfer to Durham Prison
1979	Parole refused
1980	Myra obtains BA Humanities Degree

1981	Myra's sister Maureen dies
1982	A minimum term of 25 years suggested for Myra
1983	Transfer to Cookham Wood Prison, Rochester, Kent
1983	David Astor visits Myra for first time with Reverend Peter Timms
1984	Attacked in Cookham Wood Prison
1985	Local Prison Review Committee recommends that Myra is suitable for release
1985	Parole knockback. 'Provisional' tariff of 30 years set by Home Secretary Leon Brittan
1985	Brady moved from Gartree Prison to Ashworth Special Hospital (a secure psychiatric hospital)
1986	Myra helps with (unsuccessful) search on the moors for the bodies of Pauline Reade and Keith Bennett
1987 — March	Myra returns to the moors to further help with the search
1987 — July	Pauline Reade is found
1988/89 onward	Visits with Frank Longford sporadic
1989	Berlin Wall comes down
1990	Whole life tariff set by Home Secretary David Waddington, Myra not informed of this
1992	European Single Market set up

1992	Attacked in Cookham Wood Prison
1993	Michael Howard Home Secretary
1993	Myra meets the author
1994	Secrecy of tariff system successfully challenged in the *Doody case*
1994	Howard draws up list of prisoners who in the 'public interest' would never be freed
1995	Transfer to Durham Prison
1996	Parole Board recommends Hindley for open prison
1997—February	Howard confirms her whole life tariff
1997	Jack Straw Home Secretary
1997—July	House of Lords rules that tariffs once fixed should not be increased (*Pierson case*)
1997—8 December	Judicial review of her sentence at High Court; Myra loses appeal
1998	Transfer to Highpoint Prison, Suffolk
1998	Loses appeal against life sentence in Court of Appeal
1998	Good Friday Agreement signed
2000	Loses further appeal in House of Lords (an appeal that since October 2009 would be heard by The Supreme Court).

2001	David Blunkett Home Secretary
2002 — September	Brady allowed to visit his dying mother
2002 — 15 November	Myra Hindley dies
2002 — 25 November	Ruling of Law Lords on Home Secretary and tariffs: it is incompatible with human rights for politicians rather than the judiciary to set minimum terms for lifers

Cookham Wood

"We must not forget that when every material improvement has been effected in prisons, when the temperature has been rightly adjusted, when the proper food to maintain health and strength has been given, when the doctors, chaplains and prison visitors have come and gone, the convict stands deprived of everything that a free man calls life. We must not forget that all these improvements, which are sometimes salves to our consciences, do not change that position."

Winston Churchill

CHAPTER 1

Cookham Wood

Someone shouts my name, "Nina," I look up and stare straight into the lens of a camera. This is Cornwall, 1994. The next day an outrageous and what seemed to be a maliciously fabricated article about Myra Hindley and myself would appear in *The Sun*. I had been at Cookham Wood Prison on a work placement for nearly a year when allegations were made that something improper had taken place between Myra and myself about six months earlier. One of the deputy governors suggested I take a short break while an investigation was carried out.

Despite the findings of that investigation, which completely exonerated and vindicated me, the highly damaging article made my return to Cookham Wood impossible. Prison Service Head Office decided not to take action against the newspaper, which meant that the article did not get retracted. The reason given was that this would merely give the newspaper the opportunity to rehash the whole story, only to mention at the end of it that HM Prison Service denied that there is any truth in it. Consequently, this first article was rehashed in others that would appear about Myra and myself.

On 28 October 1994 I wrote the following, this was after I received the news that I could not return to Cookham Wood Prison:

> Dear Myra,
>
> Just a quick card wondering how you are coping with this disaster. CE [the Governor] told me the news on Wednesday. The Home Office had given her a polite note telling her there was no stain on my character and asking her to thank me for the good work I had done. But that will be all, thank

you. She was also very upset and said I probably now wished I had never come to Cookham Wood in the first place. I assured her that this was not the case. I once said to her that Cookham didn't just give me work experience it also gave me life experience. And I met some very nice people there. It is shame it had to end like this, I had rather chosen the point of departure myself, but things will get better in the end.

Take care. Love Nina

Suspect by association

For years I felt the ramifications of my connection with Myra. I lost jobs whenever an article appeared about the two of us and did not get employment for the very same reason. I became tainted, suspect by association. For a long time, I had nightmares of being followed or chased. It continues to rattle on, almost 15 years after her death; there are still documentaries about her, still the occasional book and article. Because of this, I found it important to write these recollections, to make *my* voice heard. Both to set the record straight and also to describe Myra from my experience and perspective so at least a different view about her can be found within the public domain.

◊

Let me briefly describe how I arrived at Cookham Wood. I had studied criminology at the University of Amsterdam. Some time later I learnt by chance of the experimental regime at Blantyre House Prison in Kent. I approached the Governor there, who said he would be happy to have me come for a practicum; so I spent the summer months of 1993 on a placement observing "The Blantyre House Experience." There I saw that a sentence of imprisonment, even in some cases for a quite serious offence, can be served in a much more constructive way than merely being paralysed by boredom.

The keywords of Blantyre House are trust, respect, initiative and responsibility, and I concluded that if a prison sentence is to make any sense, these are the principles to be included. The choice was simple: inmates prepared for a law-abiding life outside by going on day-release to help in the community. There were various ways in which they could make themselves useful; for example, by carrying out building work, painting or helping in a residential home. If, however, they broke the rules they would get sent back to closed conditions. Prisoners would learn to confront their (offending) behaviour, and the staff at Blantyre would help them with matters such as their self-esteem, and their sometimes precarious financial independence.

The regime was unusually democratic. Inmates were involved in most decision-making. This approach makes perfect sense if you want people to return to society as well-balanced citizens; one of the inmates once said to me: "Blantyre took the bitterness out of me." The system worked, and the statistics are there to prove it. But in 2000, the prison was raided in a heavy-handed way by the police; the reason given for this drastic measure was to expose corruption. It was thought criminal activity existed in the prison and contraband was to be found. The intelligence was false and the result of the raid proved nothing, but it did lead to the destruction of Blantyre's therapeutic regime. It seems that the Home Office[1] was more concerned with how something "looked" (Blantyre could be seen as "soft") than if it worked better than standard regimes to prevent re-offending.[2]

The prison system in, for example, Sweden has, like that at Blantyre, rehabilitation and resettlement in the community at the heart of its policy, and loss of one's freedom is seen as *the* punishment. Sweden's re-offending rate is broadly speaking half that in Britain, 40 per cent; recidivism in Norway is lower still, 20 per cent. A bonus of this approach

1. Many Home Office justice-related functions are nowadays the province of the Ministry of Justice created in 2007 and headed by the Secretary of State for Justice and Lord Chancellor (a combined role). These include, e.g. general responsibility for prisons, probation and parole. The remainder of the text of this book should be read accordingly.
2. An account of the Blantyre House raid can be found in *The Blantyre House Prison Affair: Lessons From a Modern Day Witch Hunt* (2007), Murtagh, T (Foreword Narey, M), Waterside Press.

is its beneficial effect on prison staff; for, as it turns out, helping prisoners towards rehabilitation is also positive for prison officers.

The punitive approach, on the other hand, causes stress, alcoholism and hypertension amongst staff. Another big difference between Sweden (and other European countries) and Britain is the absence of the role of politicians in decision-making regarding prison policy. It is recognised there that politicians will be too much concerned with public opinion and therefore lean towards punishment instead of rehabilitation, regardless of the former's efficacy.

In The Netherlands prisons are being closed for lack of criminals and cells are leased to countries where there is insufficient cell capacity. There are various reasons for this downturn in crime. To name a few: judges are handing down shorter sentences, the population is ageing, and victimless crimes are not prosecuted. And the use of electronic tagging allows people to go back to work and remain productive members of society. Prison rehabilitation programmes are geared towards prisoners re-entering society and the focus is on job skills.

The Italian criminologist and economist, Cesare Beccaria (1738–1794), who was well ahead of his time, said that the law should be subject to the test of reason and that punishment should not be a goal pursued in its own right. The purpose of punishment is deterrence. Punishment should be imposed in order to prevent offenders from committing additional crimes. It is a tool, not an end in itself. He also said, "Crimes are more effectually prevented by the certainty than the severity of punishment." This notion, that the severity of the punishment does not make any difference in terms of recidivism, is something that so many criminologists have said and proven so many times. According to Georg Rusche and Otto Kirchheimer for example, "A constant policy of reducing the number of convictions in favour of probationary sentences coincided with a noticeable drop in the crime rate."[3] I think it was the philosopher Bertrand Russell who once compared the British penal system to a car mechanic who, instead of trying to identify the fault, treats a

3. *Punishment and Social Structure*, first published 1939. Transaction Publishers; Revised edn. (2003).

broken-down car by walking around it, kicking it and saying, "You are a very wicked car and I'm going to kick you till you go."

A defective law

One thing that I learnt at Blantyre House and seemed to get confirmed time-after-time during my work in various prisons is that the British justice system tends to be severe in its punishments of accomplices, as they are tried, indicted and punished as principal offenders under the joint enterprise laws. I have been told this policy still stems from the time of Guy Fawkes and supporters of the Gunpowder Plot.

There is now a growing voice of concern in the judiciary, academia and amongst journalists about this archaic and controversial situation. Research carried out on the doctrine concludes that this law needs to be reviewed. And indeed, there have been modern developments in that the Supreme Court has ruled that this approach is, notwithstanding earlier rulings at the highest level, incorrect.[4] This only serves to emphasise how unfair the legal position has been for so long.

Pending changes, joint enterprise is a law that allows more than one person to be charged and convicted of the same crime. Participants are, almost invariably, *unequally* culpable in fact; it was because of this that Myra Hindley could be dubbed a murderer. Although it was known she was an accessory, she was expected to assume criminal liability for Ian Brady's actions. The criticism of this law points to the fact that it can unfairly and disproportionately implicate by way of arrest, prosecution, conviction and punishment, people who are on the fringes of the actual crime as well as the central perpetrator(s). The law does not require the prosecutor to show an intent to kill someone, or that the secondary party took a direct part in the murder. The mere fact that he or she could have foreseen that a member of their group could cause someone serious bodily harm is sufficient to put them on a murder charge. This, of course, can lead to miscarriages of justice, and more than 500 people claim to have

4. See *R v Jogee* [2016] UKSC 8; [2016] WLR (D) 84.

been wrongly convicted of murder or manslaughter under this law. It is seen as a "lazy law."

You only have to look at the case of Derek Bentley, which resulted in his judicial killing in 1953, to understand how this can lead to appalling miscarriages of justice. Bentley, a teenager, but with the mental age of eleven years was involved in a botched break-in that resulted in the murder of a police officer. Christopher Craig, who fired the shot, still a juvenile at the time of the crime, served ten years in prison; Bentley, his older accomplice, was hanged. Only in 1993 was Bentley pardoned, and five years later, 46 years after the crime was committed, his conviction for murder was quashed. On this occasion, Craig spoke of his relief that Bentley's name had finally been cleared and of his regret for his actions on that day in 1952. He also apologised to his own family who had to endure years of press intrusion.

The hanging of Edith Thompson in 1923 could also only have happened with the legal backing of "joint enterprise." There was no evidence she knew that her younger lover, Frederick Bywaters, intended an attack on her husband. Her only encouragement, if it can be called that, was in highly cryptic and passionate love letters that no court would take seriously today, if it allowed them to be admitted in evidence at all. It was the slenderest of threads on which to hang someone. Edith remained confident until the end that her innocence would be recognised in time, and on the day of her execution she had to be supported by two officers to reach the scaffold and there, in the words of her counsel, was "hanged for the crime of immorality."[5]

The case of Carole Hanson is, without doubt, another example of a miscarriage of justice. Carole and her husband, Michael Hanson, were convicted in 1970 of the brutal rape and murder of ten-year-old Christine Beck. Both were sentenced to life imprisonment. Carole received a tariff of 20 years—the tariff is the minimum term (nowadays set by the sentencing judge but formerly by the Home Secretary) that "lifers" have to spend in prison before they can be considered for release—Michael Hanson confessed to his solicitor that he had only implicated Carole

5. For the most recent treatment of this iconic case that gave momentum to the campaign to end capital punishment, see *Three Cases That Shook the Law* by Ronald Bartle, 2016, Waterside Press.

because he was afraid she might have relationships with other men whilst he was in prison. He admitted to both his solicitor and Carole's defence counsel that he alone was responsible for this horrific crime.

Carole's appeal was nevertheless rejected; Lord Chief Justice Widgery stated she had been "unlucky." She was a model prisoner but was regarded as a "nonce" (sex offender) by her fellow prisoners, and had over the years received a fair amount of hassle. She did not socialise much with other inmates, keeping to herself. During my time at Cookham Wood Prison I had little contact with Carole. I did not find it easy to relate to her. I remember sitting in her cell and Carole, who was always slightly dishevelled, leaning against the wall quietly and monotonously talking to me, the air heavy and stifling. At that time I could not perceive such a travesty of justice was possible; besides, she was not the only one there who claimed to be innocent. Even so, I should have paid more attention to Carole and her story; and I did not. Usually, she had her baths in the sick bay, but on 2nd May 1997 she went upstairs to the third floor of the prison, closed the bathroom door behind her and drowned herself (the official verdict was that she died of "natural causes"). After having served 27 years in prison, Carole had simply given up hope of ever being released. Nobody had taken up her case, nobody was fighting on her behalf, she was a forgotten prisoner and unknown to the world.

◊

The English trial

The English criminal process is adversarial as opposed to inquisitorial. An adversarial system (with a judge to determine the law and the jury as finders of fact) is based on common law, that is, not necessarily codified or written but nonetheless rule bound and consisting of received traditions and the law of precedent. The judge, who acts as a kind of referee, focuses on the issues of law, and on procedure, sums up to the jury and directs them on the evidence. Trials can take a long time and are therefore costly. The barristers tend to be focused on winning, even if it amounts to avoiding and stretching the truth (which unlike the position in inquisitorial systems is not a requisite aspect of an English criminal trial as opposed to deciding guilt or innocence in legal and procedural terms). What matters can be which lawyer comes across best, and who manages to outwit whom.

David Mitchell in *The Bluffer's Guide to the Law: Bluff Your Way in Law*[6] describes it thus: "... lawyer A tries to outwit lawyer B, and the court decides on the winner by adding up points for technical merit and artistic impression." Countries with an adversarial system are, for example, England and Wales, the USA, and most former members of the old British Empire. It could be argued that an adversarial system is not doing enough to prevent miscarriages of justice. On the other hand, an inquisitorial system is based on civil law (Roman and Napoleonic), that is, written and codified and judges are bound by statutes. It is a system more interested in truth-finding and finality. The court is actively involved with the investigation, and the judge plays a pivotal role in finding the truth and evidence; he or she determines what questions to ask and ultimately decides on the information gathered. There is often no jury (though systems and exact roles and involvement vary). Countries with a court operating under the inquisitorial system are mainly to be found in continental Europe and Latin America.

◊

The Moors Murders

During my stay at Blantyre House, I visited several other prisons in Kent, one of them being Cookham Wood, a closed female establishment. HM Inspectorate of Prisons felt that Cookham Wood had the potential for a regime based on Blantyre. I believe the reasons why women commit crimes are, on the whole, different from the reasons men do, and the possibilities of rehabilitation can, therefore, be greater for women than

6. Oval Books, 2nd. revised edn. 2004.

for men. So a women's prison with a regime that corresponded with the Blantyre principles sounded like a very attractive idea to me. I approached the Governor, who told me that, when she had been put in charge of the prison, it was required that she implement some of Blantyre's ideas. I offered her my help, and she was happy to have me come on a work placement. So I started on 26 November 1993.

Before I arrived at Cookham Wood, I had only heard Myra Hindley's name a couple of times, and I vaguely remember reading an article in a Dutch newspaper about the case. When the Governor told me that Myra had been in prison for almost 30 years, I thought there must have been some mistake. In 1966 she was found guilty of her part in the "Moors Murders," so-called because at least three of the victims were buried on Saddleworth Moor in the Peak District. With her co-defendant Ian Brady, she was convicted of two murders: those of Lesley Ann Downey (aged ten) and Edward Evans (aged 17), for which she received life imprisonment. She also received a concurrent seven-year sentence as an accessory after the fact to the murder of John Kilbride (aged 12).

In 1987 she admitted her complicity in two more murders: those of Pauline Reade (aged 16) and Keith Bennett (aged 12). His body has never been found. The then Director of Public Prosecutions (DPP) decided it was not in the public interest to have a new trial and also quashed a private prosecution funded by the now defunct *News of the World.*

The tragedy of these (child) victims and the loss to their families can never be over-stated. What I have to say in this book should never be confused with or be mistaken for a lack of empathy. Criminal justice practitioners are required to somehow detach themselves from such considerations on a daily basis, to return home as normal people after dealing with some of the most notorious or difficult individuals in society. And if reason is to prevail in any sensible discussion of such matters in a bid to move on, it cannot be led by emotion however much our sympathies may lie with victims of crime or their families.

Meeting Myra

The second time I heard Myra's name mentioned was when one of the prison officers at Blantyre House told me he would be too scared to be alone in a room with her. So when I visited Cookham Wood for the first time, I was a little apprehensive about meeting this scary person, but I could not find anyone to fit the description.

The Governor took me around the prison and when back in the administration area we nearly bumped into the cleaning lady as she dragged the vacuum cleaner up the stairs. Later, in the Governor's office, someone knocked on the door and came in to give us a cup of tea. The Governor introduced us: "Myra, have you met Nina?" It was the "cleaning lady." Initially, for want of an office, I worked from the kitchen in the admin area. Myra, who worked as an administration orderly, would potter around, making tea and coffee for staff and visitors, or doing the washing-up and the vacuum cleaning. Meanwhile, I deciphered the sentence planning books.

Sentence planning was still in its infancy; it is a way to help an inmate spend his or her time in prison in the most useful way possible and with resettlement on release. It focuses on offending behaviour, but also on how to acquire skills suitable for the prisoner when back in the outside world. Because there are relatively few female prisoners compared to male prisoners, female establishments seem to be a somewhat forgotten area. Women's prisons have fewer facilities and rehabilitation programmes; consequently female prisoners tend to be insufficiently prepared for release and are less successful than male prisoners in finding employment following their time in prison. The facilities in women's establishments are also stereotypically female: I remember seeing women behind sewing-machines making tracksuits for male prisoners; there were hairdressing and cookery courses, all very much directed towards "female" jobs.

Furthermore, there is a strange contradiction that, on the one hand, many rules in women's prisons seem petty and unnecessary, and the women are often treated like children, but, on the other hand, discipline seems harsher as if better behaviour is expected from women than from men. I remember the Governor telling me that the women were not allowed perfume because it contained alcohol.

◊

My work and what I tried to achieve at Cookham Wood was not without obstacles. A group of officers was opposed to any form of change, and the fact that I spent time with Myra was regarded with suspicion. While working on sentence planning I was able to devise a more straightforward method of utilising it, and I explained what it entailed to the few officers who wanted to learn how to use it. Most officers, though, looked upon it as an unwelcome chore in addition to their other duties. Later on things improved when new officers arrived from the training school. They were enthusiastic and wanted to learn about it; they came for advice and tried to follow it through. Unfortunately, however, they met with the disapproval of and became disillusioned by the attitude of those who are described within the system as "dinosaurs." The new officers often felt intimidated to such a degree that they subsequently left their jobs; one of these officers said that everything she tried to do just got blocked by these old-fashioned officers. On the whole, the new regime the Governor tried to establish was not welcomed by the old-style prison officers, and little support could be expected from them. I also got to know the Prison Officers Association quite well, its members forever raising questions regarding security and other matters about me; it was even suggested that I was "spying" for the Governor.

On Christmas day the Governor invited Myra and me to come and play a game of Trivial Pursuit with her. Later, in the pub, I told some prison officers how I had spent my afternoon. One of them was quite amused by the thought and said, "Well, well, a Governor, a criminologist, and a murderer, playing Trivial Pursuit together."

I got on well with the majority of inmates who came to me if they needed help, for example with writing official letters, or just for a chat or a game of pool; I very much enjoyed working with them. One of the inmates told me that she dreaded her day of release and that she would much rather stay in prison. She had her friends there; she was looked after, and although being incarcerated she preferred it to life on the outside.

Vulnerable women

A lot of the inmates I met were vulnerable women; over half of women in prison report having suffered domestic violence. This is still an area that hardly gets the attention it deserves, considering that, on average, two women a week are killed by a current or former male partner. Many women in prison have mental health problems, and many are self-harmers, as was the woman already mentioned above who dreaded release. I believe a positive correlation can be found between being institutionalised and mental health problems, as the one tends to reinforce the other. And the, in my view, questionable way HM Prison Service deals with these women, is by medicating them. There was always a long queue waiting for medicines to be dispensed. Incarceration has, on the whole, a more drastic and profound effect on women than on men, psychologically and practically (including because they are frequently the primary carers of children).

Many women in prison are there because of men; they have been persuaded into committing crimes by and for their boyfriends or husbands. The irony is that the partners of male prisoners will, most of the time, be waiting for them on their release, but in my experience this loyalty cannot be found in the same way with the partners of female prisoners.

Life is bad enough for any woman in prison however short her sentence. So try to imagine what it is like for a lifer, or worse still a woman who has been told that she will never be released, or who has not been told anything at all, which is what happened to Myra for years. It is not a question of how bad her crimes may have been, rather of how any society should behave. The following quote is from *Insiders: Women's*

Experience of Prison by Una Padel and Prue Stevenson.[7] This is Sharon (a former inmate) talking:

> "I don't know how lifers cope with it, but they do. Myra Hindley has been in prison for my whole life: I'm twenty-two now, and she's been in for twenty-two years. I don't know if she'll ever get out. While I was in Cookham she got knocked back on her parole; she got a five-year review. Other people have got out, and they've done similar things to her. It was so long ago that it happened—it's an everyday occurrence now, people battering and killing children. To talk to her you wouldn't believe what she's done. She'll talk to you and give you advice and say, 'Now behave yourself, don't get into no trouble.' You wouldn't believe it. She's had some pastings while I've been away. Terrible. The way the newspapers keep writing about her just brings it all back into people's minds. Just as everyone's forgetting about Myra Hindley, there's something in the newspaper again about her."

7. Virago, 1988, p. 105.

The Outsider

"I wept as I remembered
How often you and I
Had tired the sun with talking,
And sent him down the sky."

Callimachus

CHAPTER 2

The Outsider

By not having been brought up in Britain, I had the advantage that my view of Myra Hindley was a relatively neutral one and, therefore, I could see her and appreciate her how she was when I met her, 30 years removed from the person she was when involved in those horrific crimes.

I could not *in any way* reconcile the image of the Myra portrayed by the press and media with the person I talked with daily in the prison kitchen. She was situated in sick bay at that time and therefore did not socialise much at all with other inmates; the Governor reasoned that by using the kitchen as an office I could also spend time with Myra so that she would not become too isolated, her world too small. It was also a form of compensation for the many privileges Myra did not receive. But even the few she did have were always under threat.

As already explained in *Chapter 1*, I was engaged in the then novel idea of sentence planning and that meant that I was involved in Myra's sentence plan, which had become something of a nonsense, for how do you set about sentence planning for someone like Myra who, as we shall see, had little to plan for and, as time passed, diminishing hope of release. Her priority was day-to-day survival. I was also on her lifer board. A lifer board is where various prison staff discuss a life-sentence prisoner and targets are set, for example to address offending behaviour and other long-term goals. Furthermore, it is discussed how various needs can be met through, for instance, work, education and training.

Casual interaction

And so we played board games such as Scrabble, Trivial Pursuit and Connect4, and we talked... a lot. We had many conversations on philosophy, religion, literature and almost everything else you can think of. I found Myra warm, charming and kind and felt immediately at ease with her. She was intelligent, quick-witted and had a dry sense of humour. I thought her well-read, and she loved poetry (for example Yeats). I became well-versed in poetry! Later, in HM Prison Highpoint (in Suffolk), Myra told me she wanted to do a study on the little-known poet Charlotte Mew. We gave each other books to read of which we were particularly fond; she liked to talk about what she had read; she was also a prolific and detailed writer. I found her entertaining often with some anecdote to tell. She once told me that after returning Nicolai Gogol's *Dead Souls* to the prison library, it was immediately borrowed again by an inmate, and then again and again. The librarian didn't know what was happening, Gogol had never been borrowed this often! The inmates apparently thought they could find some clue regarding Myra's crimes in this book. They must have been disappointed.

At one point she borrowed a small portable 45 rpm record player from one of the administration staff and played me some of her old records from a faded Quality Street tin. We also played a silly card game: I had a pack of cards from the National Trust with the kings and queens of England on it. I would show her one of the cards, she then had to tell me who it was, and when she *finally* got them all correct she would be released; we abandoned the game. In one of the books she gave me, she wrote: "You came at that precise junction in a life when the past is unbearable and the future uncertain"—lines from Rita Mae Brown.

"Dear Nina,

I'm writing this letter because I feel an overwhelming need to tell you what I was unable to say earlier this evening—partly because you had to leave to go to the concert. When I said you were like a breath of fresh air in my life, I meant much more than that. You are like Zephyrus, like the warm west wind [of Greek mythology], and in the short time I have known you, you have, no doubt without knowing it, blown gently away so many of the heavy, thick cobwebs that had for so long cluttered and darkened my mind, akin to drawing back the curtains in a darkened room and allowing light and sunshine to penetrate the gloom, dispelling shadows and leaving brightness and comforting warmth in their place. And I love you for this, and thank you for this—this is what I wanted to say when I kissed your cheek and said thank you as you were leaving this evening.

There is so much else that I'm grateful to you for, too much to tell you here, but I will tell you some other time. You asked me how I knew I could trust you, and I told you I just felt I could. There isn't a shadow of doubt in my mind or my heart that I can't (and I'm not crossing my fingers as I write (smile)), and it's a good and wholesome thing to feel and know, and a rare one too, for I've learned to be wary and I don't trust easily. But I feel I can talk to you about virtually everything, and above all to be myself with you—I hope I expressed this in the verse in your card. You said you aren't 'loving and giving' (Friday's child)—you are, very much so, and I'm sure there are many, like me, whose lives you have touched, who have seen and experienced those qualities you are blessed with. And I have yet another blessing to add to those which God has bestowed on me that of having met you and recognising a kindred spirit, and knowing that in such a short time you have enriched my life. You remind me of a poem [All I Ask] by D H Lawrence:

All I ask of a woman, is that she shall feel gently towards me,
when my heart feels kindly towards her,
and there shall be the soft, soft tremor as of unheard bells between us.
It is all I ask.

I hope I haven't offended you in any way by what I've written, I can only write as I feel, and as I said at the beginning, I felt the need to write.

God bless you.

Myra x"

Two cases to compare

Myra's case is not unique. I'll just mention two others with similar scenarios, where the men appeared to have exerted a Svengali-like influence over their partners. The women were corrupted over time and, in the end, became 'willing' participants in the extremely serious offences of the kidnap and murder of several victims.

One is the Bernardo/Homolka case, a pair dubbed by the Canadian media, "Barbie and Ken," because of Karla's childhood hobby of collecting Barbie dolls; the other Gallego/Williams. As in Myra's case, neither Karla Homolka nor Charlene Williams showed any criminal tendencies before meeting their boyfriends whose criminality was already established. The men are sociopaths, lacking empathy and morally and emotionally bankrupt. They try to compensate for their low self-esteem with violence and sexual sadism. The (younger) women are naïve, pathetically romantic and utterly devoted to these men. The relationship is characterised by constant duress. Systematic violence, blackmail and as already mentioned sexual sadism keep the woman in a state of (emotional) subservience, obedience and critically and—importantly—silence. Other pressure tactics used are, for example, abrupt mood swings and unpredictable behaviour; as a result, the woman is constantly "walking on eggshells," always careful not to offend or upset. The man will put her in fear of her life by real and implied threats; she will be trapped in, and paralysed by, a spiral of love, shame and fear.

Both women were involved in multiple rape/murder cases. In all three cases including Myra's, the man would commit unspeakable crimes and the woman who facilitated his acts would be described as a "willing" accomplice of him. Yet, the consistent duress, threats and emotional subjection should make us question how we define "will," and how will may be broken down by systematic and sustained abuse.

Homolka and Williams were tried separately from their boyfriends, unlike Myra, and they were lucky enough to have been tried in the 1980s, when, by that time, there was some understanding of battered women's syndrome.[1] Lawyers for both Homolka and Williams based their arguments on this syndrome and in Homolka's case Stockholm Syndrome[2] was even mentioned (as in Maggie Davis' article regarding Myra, mentioned in *Chapter 3*). Charlene Williams received a sentence of 16 years and eight months for being involved in the murder of ten children, and Karla Homolka was charged with manslaughter (following a plea bargain) and served 12 years for her part in two murders.

It could be argued that the cases involving Williams and Homolka were "worse" than Myra's, either because of the number of victims involved or, as in Homolka's case, where Karla was known to have been an active participant. Williams was released in 1997 and Homolka in 2005. Myra died in prison after serving 36 years there. How do you define justice?

Some other European comparisons

England and Wales are practically alone in handing down whole life tariffs. In Belgium, the *Dutroux case*,[3] is regarded by many as one of the worst sexual crimes in that country's history. Marc Dutroux was convicted in 2004 and sentenced to life imprisonment for the abduction, torture and rape of six girls, between 1995 and 1996, and the murder of four of them. His wife and accomplice, Michelle Martin, received a 30 year sentence for her part in the crimes. Martin helped Dutroux with the kidnap of the victims and was complicit in the starvation deaths of two of the girls when she failed to feed them whilst Dutroux was briefly in

1. Battered women's syndrome is a dissociative state caused by sustained physical, sexual and psychological abuse exercised to maintain the man's control and manipulation of the woman; some of its symptoms I have described above. It has been identified as a sub-category of post-traumatic stress disorder. Charlene Williams testified to her dissociative state when she was involved in Gallego's crimes, saying that she had been "numb," that she "did not believe any of it was really happening," and that she had been silenced afterwards by denial, fear and guilt. (*All His Father's Sins*, Ray Biondi and Walt Hecox, Prima Publishing, Rocklin, CA (1988) pp.196–204).
2. Stockholm Syndrome is a psychological scenario in which captives or hostages develop irrational feelings of empathy and sympathy for their captors; sometimes even going as far as defending them. Named after the response of hostages held for a long period during a siege following a Stockholm bank heist.
3. See https://www.theguardian.com/world/2002/jan/25/worlddispatch.dutroux

prison for an unrelated crime. She explained she was "too scared to go down into the cellar" to feed them. After serving 16 years of her sentence, Martin, "the most hated woman" in Belgium, was released from prison in 2012 and transferred to a Clarisse convent where she is to spend the rest of her sentence in prayer in atonement for her crimes.

Most European countries subscribe to Article 3 of the European Convention on Human Rights and believe that telling prisoners they will die in jail is "inhumane and degrading treatment." An average life sentence in Europe is anywhere between 12 and 25 years. Spain, Portugal and Norway don't even have a "life" sentence. Norway is the most progressive country where the maximum penalty is 21 years, however most prisoners there serve no more than two thirds of their sentence.

Holland is a strange exception; with its otherwise fairly liberal and progressive sentencing policy, it is now forced by European law to review its life sentencing system, where life indeed means life. The European Court of Human Rights has "rapped the knuckles" of the Dutch by stating there has to be a mechanism in place for treatment and rehabilitation, and only when there is risk of recidivism or when the prisoner refuses treatment, is permanent detention allowed. There should also be a mandatory point of review, after 25 years, when it will be decided if the prisoner can be released back into society, with subsequent periodical reviews.

The Nature of Myra's Injustice

"Justice is conscience, not a personal conscience but the conscience of the whole of humanity. Those who clearly recognise the voice of their own conscience usually recognise also the voice of justice."

Aleksandr Solzhenitsyn

CHAPTER 3

The Nature of Myra's Injustice

The concept and language of sexual politics were unknown at the time of the trial, and therefore unavailable to Myra Hindley and her defence team. This fact, more than any other, has contributed to the false belief that Myra Hindley committed crimes of an unparalleled awfulness.

In an article by Maggie Davis, "Myra Hindley, The Failure of British Justice,"[1] the barrister Sarah Maguire says she believes that if the insights of feminism had been around at the time the case might have been seen differently: "The lawyers might have been more imaginative and discussed with Hindley the nature of their relationship." Maguire mentions that she feels that Hindley's behaviour was profoundly affected by the relationship with Brady. She says, "Having been systematically subject to his cruelty, her mind was temporarily deranged." Stockholm Syndrome (mentioned in the last chapter) which can be seen as a form of traumatic bonding, has, according to Davis, still relevance in Myra Hindley's case, even though Myra was emotionally rather than physically kidnapped.

The writer and social commentator Beatrix Campbell (who kindly agreed to write a Foreword for this book) told BBC the Radio 4 *Today* programme that society is "absolutely" tougher on women who kill, or who are partners of murderers.

> "There's a sense in which these women are represented as 'unwomaned' by their relationship to these men, by their implication in offences against children. Meanwhile, the bigger picture of their situation is ignored. There's a story which is untold about these women. They were all targeted, enlisted

1. The article appeared in a short lived 1990s magazine called *LIP*. A copy can be obtained by writing to the author care of Waterside Press.

> as lieutenants in projects designed by men who overwhelmed them and gave them only one source of power—to protect those men's secrets. All of these women were not actually the perpetrators but they were all in the thrall, all terrified, all the servants of domineering, dangerous men. They were less transgressive than they were scared and submissive."[2]

Misogyny, blackmail and abuse

I am convinced that the treatment Myra received was largely down to misogyny. Although she had not killed, what she had done was perceived as worse *because* she was a woman. She had strayed from the allotted path and, therefore, an example had to be made of her. There is no doubt that if Brady had chosen a male accomplice he would have been paroled quietly after eight or ten years. Myra was 18 when she met Brady; she was naïve and obsessed with love for him; later this was combined with fear. In an article she wrote for the *Guardian* (18 December 1995), Myra describes her background:

> "...I grew up in what can be described as a tough working-class district where Friday and Saturday nights were known as 'wife-beating nights'; the men worked hard all week and many spent the weekends drinking."

Further along, she says:

> "Through witnessing and being on the receiving end of so much violence within my own family, I was given many lessons in dominance and control, which was probably the foundation stone on which I built my own personality."

Even after their relationship had started, Brady remained as remote and inscrutable as before and Myra felt unable to get close to him. He often vanished on jaunts of his own; and later, after Myra got her driver's

---

2. 14 May 2004.

licence, she would drive him into town where he would then disappear, often for hours, leaving her sitting in the car waiting for his return. She never knew where he had been.

She described to me how she was abused by him sexually (he subjected her to humiliating and degrading practices), emotionally and physically. Photographic evidence is (or was) also on prosecution files in the form of pornographic images taken of her[3] after she had been, so she claimed, drugged by him. He strangled her until unconscious, and he made threats on her life. When Brady started talking about his "perfect murder" Myra thought he was just fantasying again as he had been when he talked about robbing a bank. He forced her to cooperate by threatening to expose her by using the pornographic pictures he had taken of her after he had drugged her, and by making threats on her family: he said he would throw her grandmother down the stairs (she also claimed he even once drugged her grandmother just to show Myra how serious he was). He told Myra that if she backed out now and did not do what he told her, she would end up in the same grave as Pauline Reade. When Brady disappeared on to the moor with Pauline, ostensibly to "look for a glove," Myra thought of driving off and getting help. She didn't, for ultimately she feared for her family. She said in her confessions (1987), that when she became upset on seeing an appeal to Pauline to come home to her family, Brady throttled her and warned her not to show emotion like that again otherwise it would be Myra's sister next. She described how at that time: "I just wished I was dead."

It was after this first murder that Myra gave a letter to her friend May (mentioned in *Chapter 6*) saying that if she (Myra) disappeared Brady was responsible. She once told me she felt she could not do anything else but throw her lot in with his. Several times she had tried to escape, once by applying for a job at NAAFI, Women's Auxiliary Airforce. When Brady found out about this he gathered the members of her family together who then all pleaded with her not to leave them. He also made it clear in no uncertain terms to her that, if she ever tried to get away again, she would be the sorriest person alive; and she had every reason to believe him.

3. Personal communication.

The physical abuse she had sustained during her childhood meant she was used to violence and she could therefore, to some extent, take the abuse from Brady in the way she had always done in her life. It was not just her father who beat her, Myra told me her mother once hit her so hard that the next day her head was stuck to the pillow because of the dried-up blood from her ears. Myra said that she used to feel guilty for loving her gran more than her mum. Her grandmother lived more or less around the corner, so Myra could easily move between the two houses.

On 15th March 1995 Myra wrote:

> "I was lucky living with gran and Maureen living with mum and dad. All my friends had to have their little sisters and brothers tagging along with them, except me. I took Maureen out once and she fell in a swamp and came home wet through and dirty (I often did, but gran only moaned about all the extra washing I caused her); I was battered-slapped, she was coddled (she'd had a lot of illnesses and was thin and frail, whereas I was a healthy crayture (sic) and was wiry and strong) and told off..."

I never had the feeling or impression that there was anything masochistic in Myra; she simply had the ability to put up with violence. However, merely to blame her actions and omissions on Brady's abuse to her does not suffice, although this explanation obviously remains valid. But "bad relationships change good people" (Amit Verna).

Myra was an ordinary teenager, who loved swimming, dancing and reading, and who was a popular babysitter. Mrs. Joan Phillips: "She was very good. She helped teach Dennis to walk." A schoolfriend remembered her as "funny and always singing, with long, lanky hair." "She earned a reputation as a comedienne, making up ditties and telling silly jokes. She played the mouth organ" (*Daily Mail*, 7 May 1966, 'Newsight'). After having met Ian Brady, she changed dramatically. Sir William Mars-Jones, one of the prosecuting counsel at Hindley's trial, revealed to the Medico-Legal Society in 1967:

> "There was a clear distinction to be drawn between Brady and Hindley... She had been a normal, happy girl, a bit of a tomboy, who got on well with rela-

tives and friends. It was not until Brady came into her life that she suddenly began to become withdrawn and secretive and changed her whole attitude to life..."

She isolated herself from her friends, began copying Brady's opinions and even assumed his Glaswegian accent. She absorbed all his distorted philosophical theories and followed all his interests. Her greatest desire was to please him. Alix Kirsta in *Deadlier than the Male*[4] describes how Myra,

> "[I]n allowing herself to become manipulated and enthralled, body, mind and spirit, by the powerful, perverted will of her lover, [she]drifted willingly into a vast moral vacuum."

I would argue the appropriateness of using the word "willingly"; she had been persistently morally corrupted by him, and I think her relationship with Brady was so all-consuming, the abandonment of her *self* so great, that to a certain extent she had morphed into him. Thus according to Myra:

> "When I met Ian I was 18-and-a-half. He was cultured, he listened to classical music, he read classical literature. They were things that interested me too, but I had no-one to share them with. And he was good-looking. I was very impressionable. I thought I loved him, but I realise now with 20 years' hindsight that I was infatuated, and that infatuation grew into an obsession. He was God. It was as if there was a part of me that didn't belong to me, that hadn't been there before and wasn't there afterwards. I'm not saying that he took over my mind or anything, or that I wasn't responsible for what I did, but I just couldn't say 'no' to him. He decided everything; where we would go for our holidays, everything." (From *Moving Targets: Women, Murder and Representation*, Virago, 1993, p.41)

Ian Brady said at the trial:

4. Alix Kirsta, *Deadlier than the Male: Violence and Aggression in Women,* Harper Collins, 1994, p.169.

> "She was my typist in the office, I dictated to her in the office, and this tended to wrap over."

And as Myra said:

> "[A]t the age of 18, I met a man who within months convinced me there was no God at all. He could have told me that the Earth was flat, that the sun rose in the west, that the moon was made of green cheese, and I would have believed him."

She was highly romantic and completely besotted and sought to be in total union with Brady. I believe she was to a great extent emotionally hijacked. Personality change, distortion of reality and moral blindness can all be aspects of besottedness; it is a form of psychosis. Some people are willing to go to extremes for their object of infatuation, and, unfortunately, she met a homicidal maniac.

Brady's interest in pornography has already been noted. Even though he sexually assaulted at least four of his victims before murdering them, his crimes cannot be just described or dismissed as sex crimes per se; for him, it was also a way of showing his defiance of, and contempt for, society. I found it interesting to learn how Ted Bundy (one of America's most notorious serial killers) during his last interview before he was executed spoke about the connection between pornography and violence. He mentions that all the men he met in prison, who were driven to commit violence, were, without exception, influenced by an addiction to pornography. A study by the USA's Federal Bureau of Investigation (FBI) says the most common interest of serial killers is hardcore pornography.[5]

Although Myra feared Brady, she also feared losing him. To maintain her relationship with him, the suspension of her morals and beliefs had become a necessity. She followed him, and once you have crossed the line you cannot go back, you have gone too far into the abyss; and denial, lying and self-deception would be the only way to get through life.

5. FBI study (Ressler, Burgess and Douglas, 1988) which revealed that of 36 interviewed and researched serial killers 29 of them were attracted to pornography, and it showed how they incorporated this addiction into their criminal sexual activity, including serial rape-murder.

Again, according to Myra:

> "And I never was actually led to the realisation that Ian Brady was a sadistic killer; certainly not before I came to prison. I simply didn't know whether he [was] or not."

It does not seem strange to me that her mind refused to comprehend the enormity of the crimes; she lived in a complete state of denial and this was probably the only way for her to protect her sanity. Myra was quoted as saying, "I didn't think about what I had done at all, it was too terrible to contemplate... I was no help to the police then, I just shut off my mind." (*The Sunday Times*, 18 December 1994)

For the first few years in prison she was still very much under Brady's influence, and the fact that it took her so long to extricate herself from his domination illustrates the extent of the hold he had over her. Yet, in prison she had to retain a moral detachment from the events to survive in much the same way that she had had to with Brady. And lies would have been the only way to save face.

After nearly 20 years in prison, Myra received some form of counselling. There she confessed to the full extent of the crimes and also *her* role in them; this was in the mid-1980s. In 1986 Myra received a letter that profoundly distressed her and to which she wanted to respond; it was from the mother of Keith Bennett (written by a journalist), who begged Myra for her help and asked her to tell what had happened to her son. In the meantime, Greater Manchester Police decided they wanted to reopen the case, this because Brady had started talking about two more murders. In 1987, Myra "officially" confessed to these two further murders. The Home Office then made the incredible and harsh decision to stop her counselling. An incomprehensible decision, for one would have thought that any form of understanding of why Myra had got involved in these crimes would have been beneficial not solely to her but would also have provided an invaluable insight for others.

After owning up to these murders and making a full confession, she wrote to the authorities asking them not to consider her for parole when her next scheduled review came up in 1990. Her explanation is encapsulated by the following:

> "I knew what we were doing was wrong. But I can't explain it. When we were arrested, it was a relief, although I couldn't admit it to myself at the time. I was so terrified, and what we'd done was so terrible. For years I just blocked it; I couldn't talk about it or even admit it to myself. When I made the confession it was as if a weight had been lifted. I just wish I could have done it 20 years before. The wounds began to heal, then my counselling was cut off, and I was left with the enormity of what I'd done, but I couldn't go any further. I tried writing it all down, but apart from the fact that I could only write in privacy at night when we were locked up and I had terrible nightmares, I didn't understand it myself. I feel a terrible guilt. It's as if the wound opened up and then scarred over but the pain was still there. There is still a blockage. I just wish I could explain it somehow." (From *Moving Targets: Women, Murder and Representation*, Virago, 1993, p. 59).

◊

Myra on 2 January 1995:

> "I remember the night I was 'sent for' about my tariff (I expect someone at Head Office phoned to arrange a 'pick up' time at the prison. Maybe they, HO and prison left it until late evening so it wouldn't be noticeable, although (someone) on the gate wouldn't fail to know it was something 'strange' for a courier to arrive and be met by CE [the Governor]; when she told me as I went in (her) office that it was about my tariff and there were no surprises—meaning it was what I expected it to be, I asked her to read the letter to me as I didn't have my specs with me. She reached a part which I wanted her to read again, and I realised that PM [one of the deputy governors] was sitting watching my expression—which hadn't changed, and it reminded me of when Topping (Chief Superintendent) and Mr Knupfer (Detective Superintendent) used to always come to see me together. Often, when Topping was talking, I raised my eyes to find George

> Knupfer watching my face. I don't know why I waffled on about that, and I'm sure you don't either.
>
> It's 2.30 Monday afternoon…It's Brady's birthday—I'm not celebrating (smiley)—I think he's 56—I was reminded, listening to the news at 1.0 and having read the Guardian, which disappointed me, again, by devoting the front page and pages 2 + 3 to F. [Frederick] West, that he, I. B., was going to commit suicide on remand, and I begged him not to. What an idiot I was. He put off an escape plot too—so he said; there were several escapes while we were at Risley."

It was not always understood how Myra Hindley could keep many of her feelings to herself in the way she did. I think people expected more emotions, more tears, shock or anger. I seldom saw her angry, not often enough in my view (she once jokingly told me that if *I* had been in prison I would be constantly down the "block" (punishment)).

It could seem as if she was untouched by things; she described it as a defence mechanism that was now part of her. She told me she just reacted to situations and then put her feelings on hold to deal with when alone. In a way this "self-control" helped her "survive" her sentence for as long as she did, but naturally it also worked against her. An explanation for this "shielding" could be, apart from pride and dignity, a life-long training: from a young age onwards she had learnt to keep her emotions under control and only cry in private. I sometimes felt, though, that either out of habit or necessity she might have buried her emotions so deep that even for herself they had become inaccessible. This was the reason why I eventually, to a certain extent, drifted away from her. People have commented with surprise on the fact she had so few hang-ups, but the suppression of her deepest feelings had, of course, an effect, seemingly positive in the case of not having many hang-ups.

◊

Myra did not actively participate in the murder of any child, and she has always been consistent in saying she never harmed any of the children, physically or sexually. She did under the kind of influences already described, lure children for Brady. Yet in the case of the last child victim, Lesley Ann Downey, Myra's involvement was greater and more damning than in any other case. Myra's voice can be heard on a tape-recording, first trying to quieten the child, finally panicking and telling her to "shut up." Myra was present when Brady took indecent pictures of the girl, but denies being present when the child was sexually assaulted and then strangled by him. I know that she was haunted by her actions and that she was desperately struggling to come to terms with her involvement in the crimes, and, as she told me, to come to some form of understanding of the "Why?"

In HM Prison Highpoint she asked me if I could find her a psychotherapist, which I did, and she started to write about Brady's maltreatment of her and described doing so as being cathartic:

> "...and whilst it often traumatises me when I'm writing-typing—at the same time it's a means of bringing everything out of me that I've 'hidden' for years, and brings a measure of relief.
>
> It reads like a horrible horror story as I remembered more and more things."

Because Myra had to find a way of funding the psychoanalyst first, the psychotherapy only started in 1999. Perhaps this should have been available to her at the beginning of her sentence.

Public and Political Involvement

"And all these people wanted was a fun day out, right? Atticus ruins everything with his fair, reasonable, and calm approach to deciding a man's fate. Spoilsport."

"The courtroom spectators get what they came for with Mr Ewell: sex, scandal, and hate-mongering. This isn't a crowd ready to listen to reason."

(Both quotes from) *To Kill a Mockingbird* by Harper Lee

CHAPTER 4

Public and Political Involvement

"Hindley was convicted as an accessory to two murders in 1966 and is still in prison. She was not physically present at four of the five killings, withdrawing upstairs to the bathroom while Lesley Ann Downey was strangled, and otherwise busying herself parking their van as Brady guided the children across the moors to their doom. Nor did she strike their last victim Edward Evans. Hindley has now served almost the harshest sentence of any killer since the abolition of capital punishment, and if standard parole rules were applied to her case, she would be eligible for release. But the Home Office's freedom of action is uniquely circumscribed by public opinion." Oliver Cyriax, *The Penguin Encyclopaedia of Crime* (1996)

Justice versus politics

For justice to prevail there cannot be public or political involvement in how it is delivered (as opposed to the administrative arrangements for it to actually be provided and exist at all). Both tend to have baser interests and instincts, especially insofar as public opinion is represented by the media with its priority of selling news (see *Chapter 6*). One of the principles of justice, English or otherwise, is that all are equal before the law; everyone no matter who they are or what they have been alleged to have done is entitled to objective, fair and equal treatment. And it must not be inhuman or degrading (or worse—amount to torture).

One thing that struck me more than anything else was the fact that the Home Secretary had the quasi-judicial power to release (or not to release) those who were sentenced to life imprisonment, and also to extend tariff dates, often going against the decision and advice of the trial judge and the Lord Chief Justice.

This constitutional anomaly has since been largely corrected but during Myra's sentence the Home Secretary was responsible for both law and order and the administration of the prisons including post-sentence review of punishments. It was often commented that no Home Secretary would risk his or her political future by releasing Myra Hindley and she became a kind of totem of the resolve of those occupying that position. Although much of what follows has now been affected by legal changes and shifts in responsibility, it is sound for the time that Myra was in prison and the issue of her release in the public eye. The European Court of Human Rights ruled in 2015 that British courts have the right to impose a whole life tariff provided that release is possible in "exceptional circumstances" such as when justified on grounds of compassion. In other words life can indeed still mean life.[1]

About 300 years ago the French lawyer and political philosopher Charles Louis de Secondat, Baron de Montesquieu (1689–1755), wrote an extensive work, *The Spirit of the Laws* in which he pointed out the necessity for the separation of the three arms of state: the Legislature, the Executive and the Judiciary. De Montesquieu was influenced on the subject by writers from England, and borrowed some of their ideas. One of them was the philosopher John Locke, who had already written on the topic. De Montesquieu expanded and improved on the such points, especially their judicial aspects. The danger of what can happen when powers are not separated was clearly to be seen in Myra Hindley's case; as other elements than the judicial will proceed to dictate the course of events, emotions often taking over. A politician who is (necessarily) influenced by votes (or the next ballot), cannot possibly "speak" true justice. As De Montesquieu poignantly put matters: "Justice cries out loud, but its voice is barely heard in the tumult of passions."

The reason why some such judicial powers lay in the hands of the Home Secretary was down to a fluke in history. The royal prerogative of mercy was a power of English monarchs stemming from ancient times.

1. See *Hutchinson v. United Kingdom* (Application No. 57592, February 3, 2015).

They used it to show mercy by pardoning offenders (Royal pardon). It was also applied to redress miscarriages of justice. When Queen Victoria ascended to the throne in 1837 at the age of 18, she was deemed to be too young and politically innocent to be in charge of such a worldly mandate. Parliament decided to delegate the power to the Home Secretary.

The distinction between Brady and Hindley

At the "trial of the century" at Chester Assizes, Hindley's QC, Godfrey Heilpern, pleaded for severance of the cases of Ian Brady and Myra Hindley. The trial judge, Mr Justice Fenton Atkinson, however, decided it should be "left to the jury" to disentangle the complexities of what were two separate cases with widely differing degrees of involvement and guilt. Heilpern's later appeal was based on Hindley not having being allowed a separate trial.

> "There was so much vital, fundamental evidence going to the whole root of the question of Brady's guilt, which was evidence against him and not evidence against her ... It was impossible for a direction to have been given to the jury which would have realistically enabled them to go through the mental gymnastics involved and to separate the cases in their minds."[2]

After Brady and Hindley were convicted of murder, Fenton Atkinson refrained from recommending a tariff, that is the respective minimum term both should serve. In his letter to the Home Secretary of May 1966, he did, however, make a clear distinction between Brady and Hindley. He wrote:

> "Though I believe that Brady is wicked beyond belief without hope of redemption (short of a miracle), I cannot feel that the same is necessarily true of Hindley once she is removed from his influence."

2. *The Times*, 18 October 1966.

Further along he continues:

> "I hope Brady will not be released in any foreseeable future (assuming his fellow prisoners allow him to live) and that Hindley (apart from some dramatic conversion) will be kept in prison for a very long time."

"A very long time" is indeterminate, of course; but what it clearly *is not*, is forever, or a whole life term. To give an example of what was seen, by some senior members of the judiciary, as "a very long time," here is the trial judge sentencing Peter Sutcliffe (the Yorkshire Ripper) in 1981:

> "I am recommending a minimum sentence of 30 years. That is a long period, an unusually long period in my judgment, but you, I believe, are an unusually dangerous man."

Sutcliffe attacked at least 20 women, killing 13 of them, he claimed it was the voice of God ordering him to kill.

When the Home Office sought the opinion of Lord Chief Justice, Lord Widgery in 1978 he said:

> "As to any distinction between Brady and Hindley, I think that it will be widely expected that the woman will serve a shorter term."

In 1982, the Lord Chief Justice, Lord Lane wrote that he would never release Brady:

> "[T]his is a case, if ever there is one, when a man should stay in prison until he dies."

He mentions, as the trial judge had already pointed out, that there were material differences between the cases of Brady and Hindley. He recommended that she serve a minimum of 25 years. He confirmed this advice in 1985.

The final decision of the ultimate tariff, which would normally be no longer than was judicially advised, was, however, at that time left to the Home Secretary and was reached in strict secrecy; the prisoner was not informed of the reasoning and could only guess at the tariff's length.

A fruitless recommendation for parole

In 1985 the Local Review Committee (LRC) recommended Myra Hindley's release to the Parole Board (every single report). Their reasoning was she had "confronted her offending behaviour and was no risk to the public." In spite of this the board, under the chairmanship of Lord Windlesham, gave her an unprecedented five-year knockback. He was said to be unhappy about the decision and it was rumoured to be a three to two majority "verdict." The board did, however, recommend her speedy release in 1991, "without prior public notice." Instead, Leon Brittan, the then Home Secretary, quietly increased her tariff to the "provisional" 30 years. It was a term not heard of before and no-one could know what it was supposed to be "provisional" upon. Myra had, by then, served 19 years, well over the normal life term. The following is an extract from a copy of Myra Hindley's petition dated 4 June 1985 to Brittan regarding the five-year knock-back.

> "...I heard you being interviewed on BBC Radio Four's PM news programme. The woman who interviewed you said she could not understand why the date for the next review had been set so far ahead. Your reply was that the public would understand. As I wrote in my representation to the Local Review Committee and repeated this to the lady who interviewed me, I feared they were wasting their time submitting a report on me, as were those in Cookham Wood, because I believed you would never sanction a release for political reasons. But if risk is the pre-eminent factor determining release, and I am not a risk to the public, why did you uphold an unprecedented five-year 'knock-back'? So that like Pilate you could wash your hands of my case, for that length of time?...You also say in the Parole Board Report, p.10. that you look to the judiciary for advice on the time to be served to satisfy the requirements of retribution and deterrence, and 'I will decide the date of a first reference of a case to a Local Review

Committee following the initial consultation with judiciary.' I take this to mean that you consulted the Lord Chief Justice (I assume my trial judge is no longer alive), and he gave his opinion about how long I should serve before being released. Was this information conveyed to the Parole Board before they considered my case? ... With regard to the matter of retribution, if my co-defendant and I were to be separated in your mind, those of the Parole Board (I know our cases are considered separately, but the link between us is inextricable since we were tried together), the Lord Chief Justice, the media and the public, retribution should take on a different aspect and be a separate issue, as would culpability.

Not only were our charges different (mine were changed three times, the last time only minutes before the trial began), our convictions were too. In his summing-up, the trial judge stressed to the jury that there were many allegations made against my co-defendant that were not made against me; he had also made many admissions that I had not made, and the judge urged the jury to separate us completely when considering their verdicts. How could they when there had been seven months of media brainwashing prior to the trial, and we'd stood together in the dock for three weeks?

Hence the incongruity of the concept of retribution (...........) In June 1977, at a Press conference to mark the publication of the Parole Board's annual report, the Chairman—and I quote from a letter dated June 28th of that year, from the Secretary of the Parole Board, replying on behalf of the Chairman to an earlier letter of mine, was asked to comment on the impact of public opinion on the Board's consideration of 'notorious cases', and made it quite clear that in his view the Board must give it full weight; if it did otherwise and made a recommendation which outraged public opinion the future of the whole Parole system could be prejudiced ..."

Myra wrote the following to a friend of mine:

"Just as a matter of interest, after a debate in the House of Lords on whether to abolish the mandatory life sentence and replace it with a determinate sentence made by the judge at trial after conviction, the vast majority deci-

> sion was in favour of it (The Commons overruled it of course). Waddington, now Lord Waddington, Leader of the House, voted against it. At that time, life-sentences were part of the then Criminal Justice Act. Waddington was asked why he voted against it, and he replied that for the most heinous of murders—obviously referring to 'The Moors Murders'—a very long sentence would have to be imposed, e.g. 60 years, of which 30 must be served, and he knew of no judge who had imposed 60 years. Ironically, when he gave me a 5 year knock-back in 1990 (August) he actually 'sentenced' me to 60 years—in 1995 I would have served 30."

But worse was yet to come. In 1990, David Waddington, the then Home Secretary, fixed a "whole life" tariff for Myra Hindley without informing her (again this sentence, "whole life," just like the "provisional tariff," did not exist in law). "The whole-life tariff is the construction of successive Home Secretaries since 1988; it is a creature of executive policy, described as 'illogical and misleading.'"[3]

In 1994 a murder convict named Doody challenged the secrecy of the tariff system and won his case.[4] He argued he should be told what tariff was recommended by the judiciary, and any departure from this by the Home Secretary. He also stated that he should be given the reasons of both judicial and Home Office views. The Law Lords agreed with him and declared that disclosure was of paramount importance to prisoners as it was also a way of exposing any errors or abuses. This meant that Myra Hindley, and others, had to be told their tariffs too. This posed a problem for Michael Howard QC (by then Home Secretary) for he could not, by any stretch of the imagination, claim that she constituted such a public risk that her continued incarceration was justified.

Yet, being a public risk would be the only excuse he had to keep her in prison. A month after the Doody case, Howard declared a new element, apart from retribution and deterrence, determining the release dates of lifers, namely the notion of *public acceptability*. He announced that he had drawn up a list of murderers who in the "public interest"

---

3. Extract from a letter to *The Times* by Professor Terence Morris and Louis Blom-Cooper QC dated 5 January 1998.
4. *R v Secretary of State for the Home Department, ex parte Doody* [1994] 1 AC 531.

would never be released. He explained that, in making his decision, he had taken account of "the public mood," that is, whether people find someone's release "acceptable," regardless of their being no danger to society. In other words, a prisoner's release could become dependent on the Home Secretary's assessment of the nation liking you or not.

This was no doubt an expression of Michael Howard's wish to give society the justice system it "yearns for," yet by doing so he was negating the whole point of *having* a justice system. As the whole life list was not made public (despite the alleged public interest), and initially the only person known for certain to be on it was Myra Hindley, it seemed as if the only reason for the existence of it was to accommodate Prisoner 964055 Myra Hindley; more so, as it is mostly the criminally insane who are detained for the rest of their natural lives, and who gradually appeared on Michael Howard's list once it was known; and they are not in a prison, but in a secure hospital such as Rampton, Broadmoor or Ashworth.[5]

Many penal reformers, I think, believed that Britain's life-sentencing system had been designed specifically with Hindley in mind. Her incarceration had become a moral issue instead of a judicial one. Sir Ivan Lawrence QC (formerly an MP), apparently declared on BBC *Newsnight* in 1995: "We listened to public opinion in the case of Myra Hindley, didn't we?" Just reminding us how politically motivated her continued incarceration was. As an example of how far this went, Myra wrote to me on 24 March 1997:

> "It is Sunday afternoon; I've just watched the Jonathan Dimbleby programme which was on crime and punishment, with Howard (Tory), Straw (Labour) and Alan Beath (Liberal Democrats). I knew I would be mentioned, and I was . . . Howard was asked by a man in the audience what would happen if the ECHR recommended my release, and Howard strongly implied — in fact he said — that if this was the case, Britain would probably withdraw as signatories!"

5. When the list was made public in 2006, Peter Sutcliffe was not even on it. Only in 2010 did he receive a whole life tariff.

Howard's "policy" was heavily criticised by some senior judges, the most well-known being Lord Woolf,[6] Lord Donaldson[7] and Lord Taylor of Gosforth, as it made nonsense of judicial sentencing and a farce of impartial justice.

In 1995, Myra had been visited by the Parole Board, and in 1996 it was disclosed that they had recommended her transfer to an open prison. The reasoning behind it was that she had "confronted her offending behaviour and was no risk to the public." Were it not for Howard's ruling of "public acceptability," her parole should have been a formality. But again this term would not even allow her such a move, and she stayed exactly where she was, at that time in top security Durham Prison.

In February 1997, her whole life tariff was confirmed by Michael Howard. Before this was officially announced the decision was "leaked" to the *Daily Mail*, whose gloating headline was, "Hindley Will Never Go Free." It was down to Ann Widdecombe (former Minister of Prisons) to justify the natural life term conferred on Myra Hindley.

Newark-on-Trent
4 February 1997

Dear Ms Widdecombe[8]

You had the grace to look quite uncomfortable on television today, as you tried to explain the Home Secretary's decision about Myra Hindley.

I am writing to you and not the Home Secretary because I have no reason to expect any understanding of conscience whatsoever from the present Home Secretary.[9] On the other hand, we heard a great deal recently about your own (Christian) conscience. That makes it appropriate to remind you of a statement that Shirley Williams made when she had the shadow brief

6. Lord Woolf described Howard's policies as "shortsighted and irresponsible," involving "knee-jerk decisions off the top of his head."
7. On 3 November 1995, Lord Donaldson said on BBC *Newsnight*: "What I would dispute is whether sentencing in individual cases should be based on public opinion. That, in my view, is mob rule."
8. Ann Widdecombe was Minister of State for Prisons from 28 February 1995 to 2 May 1997.
9. Michael Howard.

for Home Affairs. She said that in the event of Labour (her then party) winning a forthcoming general election, she would not be a candidate for Home Secretary because there remained a possibility of capital punishment being applied. She said she had taken that decision to avoid any conflict between her departmental duty and her Catholic faith.

Now, Ms Widdecombe, you pushed your Christian conscience up our noses not so long ago, courting publicity for your conversion to Catholicism. So what is the difference between hanging someone and imprisoning someone for life? Apart from the fact that the resolving of any miscarriage of justice becomes a bit more practical? Either course assumes that the sinner is beyond redemption on this earth.

You have attempted to justify the unique tariff for Miss Hindley by reference to her crimes. So far as there is any purpose in ranking one murder worse than another—and it was you that chose this argument—her crimes were not the worst of the past 30 years, as well you know. They were probably not even equal with the worst. No wonder you squirmed today and chose your words with such cynical care.

Remember the Manchester girl[10] who was starved and tortured over a period of days; set on fire, and thrown onto a rubbish dump, where she continued to endure life for a few more hours? Who were her assailants? Ask in the street and nobody knows.

10. Suzanne Capper (aged 16) was murdered in 1992. After having been tortured for days, she was doused with petrol and set alight. She had over the course of nearly a week been subjected to the most horrific acts of violence. Capper had her hair and eyebrows shaved off, was beaten and kicked, and suffocated with a plastic bag. Two of her front teeth were pulled out with pliers, and she was put in a bathtub with undiluted disinfectant and scrubbed with a brush that took off her skin. Amongst her assailants were the instigators Bernadette McNeilly (aged 24), Jean Powell, now reverted to Gillespie (aged 26) and Jean's ex-husband, Glyn Powell (aged 29). They were sentenced to life imprisonment with a minimum tariff of 25 years. On appeal, McNeilly had her sentence reduced by one year. A model prisoner, McNeilly was released early, in 2014; at court, it was heard she had made 'exceptional progress' in prison. The perpetrators of this crime possibly benefitted from the fact that their trial coincided with the James Bulger case and, therefore, had received relatively little attention.

The name of Jason Swift[11] does seem to have lingered in some people's memories. But who killed him? And who led that dreadful paedophile gang in Homerton? Again you can ask around, and no-one knows.

And what about 'Johnny come Home' the Yorkshire TV documentary and book about the horrific fate of some homeless youngsters in London? I expect that's long forgotten as you calculate the unique horror of Miss Hindley's crimes. But then 'Johnny come Home' was 20 years ago …

But you know all these arguments better than anyone. And you know (because Lord Longford has said it so many times, and said it again today) that the only unique thing about Miss Hindley is the way in which an irresponsible press has turned her into a national pariah.

So Bravo Ms. Widdecombe. You have expressed the populist lynch-mob line with great courage. A true leader.

But I wonder: is there any issue at all on which that trumpeted Christian conscience of yours could ever persuade you to resign your precious toehold in government? As you too ponder this, you might find the Ballad of Reading Gaol a helpful read, dripping as it is with New Testament references that will resonate with your Christian soul. Four lines, in particular, come to mind:

'… *every prison that men build*
Is built with bricks of shame
And bound with bars lest Christ should see
How men their brothers maim.'

Yours sincerely,

---

11. During the 1980s Robert Oliver was a member of a paedophile ring that abducted, gang-raped and murdered children and buried them in shallow graves. Oliver was convicted of the killing of 14-year-old Jason Swift and was implicated in the deaths of two others, including that of Mark Tildesley, aged seven, who was lured away from a fair. Oliver was released after serving eight years of a 15 year sentence. He was re-arrested in 2013 for breaching a sexual offences prevention order, and re-released in 2014. Paedophiles have a high rate of recidivism.

Peter Kirker

PS. I enclose a stamped addressed envelope in case you might be able to tell me how I can make contact with Miss Hindley. I thought I might send her a note just to remind her that some of us beyond the wall are revolted by the treatment she has had to endure from the state and from the press."

A press statement on behalf of Myra Hindley responded to Michael Howard's decision by making the following points: it had failed to reflect the views of all the judiciary consulted in her case that she serve less than her co-defendant, Ian Brady. Also, that this decision demonstrated that Michael Howard had bowed to political pressure and public opinion rather than considering the merits of her case. Furthermore, it represented an unjustifiable and irrational leap from the 30 year period originally fixed by the Home Secretary in 1985. It also failed to take into account her exceptional progress in prison and genuine remorse. And it fettered the Home Secretary's discretion to release her conferred by section 35(2) Criminal Justice Act 1991.

In May 1997 Myra was given the go-ahead to have her Waddington/Howard tariff judicially reviewed. The purpose of such a review is to settle points of law and to establish the lawfulness of decisions made and actions taken by a public body. The main point of law in this case was to establish if Michael Howard had acted illegally by upholding the increased tariff of Myra Hindley and whether Jack Straw had done likewise in verifying this decision. When New Labour Home Secretary Jack Straw came to power he had an opportunity to rid himself and every subsequent Home Secretary from "the Myra Hindley problem" by implementing the cross-party parliamentary Home Affairs Select Committee report of December 1995, and to repeal his power over sentencing. The report recommended that power over individual sentencing be removed from Home Office jurisdiction, and that it should be placed in the hands of the judiciary where it belongs. A move that would have undoubtedly been welcomed by everyone who values justice. But he didn't. Instead of rightfully condemning the personal and populist policies of his predecessor, Straw stressed that he had no intention of relinquishing his right to "the final say over release dates" and also defended his right to "consider public feeling."[12]

In July 1997 the House of Lords had upheld a judgement regarding the judicial review of murder convict John Pierson: tariffs, once set, should not be increased. Pierson had challenged the fact that his tariff had been increased from 15 to 20 years. The Law Lords ruled the Home Secretary had no general power to increase a tariff once fixed *and communicated*, because it "conflicted with the elementary legal principles of fairness."[13] Jack Straw claimed that the House of Lords judgment

> "...does not directly affect the date on which an individual having served the tariff is released, or whether indeed, in some cases, they will ever be released"!

In November of the same year it was "leaked" that Jack Straw had confirmed the Waddington/Howard decision. His timing for his public announcement seemed calculated, it being only weeks before Hindley's appeal was heard. In terms of fairness and impartiality his pre-emption of the High Court ruling was, in my view, shameful.

A month later the decision of the court regarding Myra Hindley's case was, although clearly marked "confidential to counsel," yet again "leaked" to the *Daily Mail.* Their headline: "Hindley Freedom bid Quashed."[14]

Howard's detention ruling that prevented prisoners gaining release by virtue of their exceptional progress in prison or their clear lack of dangerousness, was judged unlawful because it bound the Home Secretary's own discretion. Straw, however, had stayed within the law by stating he would be open to the possibility of "exceptional progress." So, although Straw had ruled Myra Hindley would never be freed, he had not ruled out her release in future! Yet with regard to the applicant's tariff, Howard had acted within the law because Myra Hindley's tariff suggested by Lord Lane, increased by Leon Brittan, once more increased by David Waddington and confirmed by Howard, had not been fixed. It was a

12. News broadcasts and BBC2 *Newsnight* 24 July 997 in response to the House of Lords judgment the *Pierson case.*
13. *Regina v. Secretary of State for the Home Department, ex parte Pierson,* 27 July 1997.
14. *Daily Mail,* 18 December 1997.

"provisional" tariff (a term described as "unusual" by Lord Bingham). Hindley had anyway not been informed of her tariff, and unless this had been communicated to her it was not a real tariff at all, even if it had been intended as such.

An increasingly Kafkaesque situation

Myra seems to have received "justice" straight out of Kafka: if you have been told your tariff, it cannot be changed, but if, for whatever dubious reasons, the state decides not to inform you, your tariff can be expanded *ad infinitum*! Whatever became of the legal principles of fairness, openness and equality? Not to mention another principle of English law

> "…Nor shall a heavier penalty be imposed than the one that was applicable at the time the criminal offence was committed."

Hindley, the accessory, had by now been in prison for 31 years.

Moving the goalposts

So for Myra Hindley the goalposts had been removed altogether, and as her counsel Edward Fitzgerald QC pointed out to the judges this was the only case of "whole life" in which the offender was not the actual killer. Moreover, she had committed her offences under duress. Fitzgerald added: "One of the suspicions one harbours is that this applicant may have been singled out because of her particular notoriety."

She was also the only prisoner whose crimes, over the years, remained firmly in the eyes of the media, press and the public whose supposed "opinion" became reflected in high profile polls, for example:

- in 1985, *The Sun*: 86 per cent opposed her being paroled;
- in 1989, *Kilroy*, BBC 1: 94 per cent opposed her freedom;
- in 1994 in a BBC telephone poll: 96 per cent thought she should not be released; and

- Teletext on 14 October 2000: 6606 people responded to the poll question "Should Myra Hindley be released?" 93 per cent said no. (Next poll question was "What is your favourite Cliff Richard hit?").

And similarly other hardening attitudes:

- Teletext polls, 1995: 92 per cent were for corporal punishment, 85 per cent for hanging, 47 per cent thought hanging innocent people (by way of mistake one assumes) was acceptable!
- In 1999, 90 per cent of the public had no confidence in the justice system. However, 86 per cent were then still for hanging!

And apparently also for the Home Office, her offences had become gradually worse. She had served three times the then average life sentence, she was regarded as a model prisoner and posed no threat to the public. She had certainly satisfied the criteria expected by the law, namely that of punishment, deterrence and rehabilitation. I believe her sentence had become a "cruel and unusual punishment."

Here is another example of the somewhat cavalier approach of the judiciary to someone else's liberty. Lord Denning, former Master of the Rolls: "It is better an innocent man serves a life sentence than the law is seen to be making grave errors." He also said, "[M]y opinion is, that it is more important to uphold public confidence in our system of justice than to allow convicted (alleged to be innocent) people to go free." (A reference to the Birmingham Six).[15]

This is a far cry from what the English jurist William Blackstone said, that to protect the legitimacy of the fundamental principle of our system of justice, "It is better that ten guilty persons escape than that one innocent suffer."[16]

Benjamin Franklin upped the ratio: "That it is better a hundred guilty persons should escape than that one innocent person should suffer, is a

15. It was strange to see Lord Denning, a judge who did much to protect the vulnerable, to act judicially in the interest of the "common man and woman," reveal a reluctance to admit of judicial fallibility when he expressed the view that once a judge and jury had dealt with a case, journalists should not be poking their noses in." http://www.legalweek.com/legal-week/blog-post/2041209/rough-justice-lord-denning-illiberal-judiciary
16. *Commentaries on the Laws of England*, 1765.

maxim that has been long and generally approved" (Letter to Benjamin Vaughan, 1785).

In 1830, Robert Peel, when Home Secretary, wrote:

> "It is impossible to conceal from ourselves that capital punishments are more frequent and criminal law more severe on the whole in this country than any other country in the world."

Children, for minor offences, would go to the gallows to the discredit of the entire justice system. The English were notorious for their readiness to hang prisoners. In 1846, the writer William Makepeace Thackery wrote about an execution: "I feel myself ashamed and degraded at the brutal curiosity which took me to that brutal sight… It seems to me that I have been abetting an act of frightful wickedness… I came away that morning with a disgust for murder, but it was *for the murder I saw done*."

Just like today, England is well-known for the large number of people it sends to prison. Percentage-wise more people are sent to British prisons than in most other Western European countries. And the sentences meted out here are on the whole also longer. England has more life sentence prisoners than the whole of Western Europe put together. A life sentence is now (2016) on average 17 years, in 2001 it was 13, three decades ago it was on average ten years.[17]

17. Prison Reform Trust, "Prison: The Facts", Bromley Briefings, Summer 2016.

Reputation, Retreat and Remorse

"Nothing can be more abhorrent to democracy than to imprison a person or keep him in prison because he is unpopular. This is really the test of civilisation."

Winston Churchill

CHAPTER 5

Reputation, Retreat and Remorse

Because it has so often been suggested that Myra was manipulative, I have naturally reflected on this extensively, and I tried to think back to see if I ever felt this was the case, but during the eight years I knew her I never felt manipulated by her; on the contrary, she could have asked me to do much more for her, but she never did, always keeping my welfare in mind.

I once was invited to appear on a television programme to argue in her favour, I declined. Myra was glad I had not accepted, fearing how this could have affected *me*. If anything, I found her sometimes rather naïve, too readily trusting of people; she was prey to several con merchants. If she *was* a manipulator, she was extraordinarily bad at it. You only have to look at her behaviour just after Ian Brady got arrested and at her conduct at the trial. During the four days of liberty, before she was herself arrested she was mainly to be found at the police station asking after Brady's wellbeing and wanting to see him, and when on her arrest the police asked her to explain what had happened, she replied, "What did Ian say?" He, on the other hand, seemed to try to find ways to protect himself. First of all, he instructed a solicitor to act for both of them, and later he suggested they marry. On both occasions, Myra interpreted this as a gesture of concern and care for her. It is, of course, more likely that Brady, no doubt knowing full well how Myra could stitch him up, tried to make certain she could not testify against him. He might have been disparaging about marriage before then, but he was probably aware of the strength of the marital privilege evidentiary rule as it then stood.

Whatever the case, the Home Office, perhaps suspicious of Brady's motives, denied the request. Her wretched loyalty to Brady and her impassive demeanour at the trial did her great harm. The expressionless "mask" was a form of defence: the public gallery was full, and the scrutiny of the visitors in the courtroom was intense. Myra told me she even saw people peering at her through theatre binoculars.

She could have helped her case enormously if she had shown more emotion, her barrister had even said to her that "a few tears wouldn't go amiss." Also, if Myra had stated how Brady had terrified and blackmailed her. But she did not, and this was a testament of her feelings for him, misguided as they were. With a hastily scribbled note she even stopped her barrister with his line of questioning, whenever he tried to establish how Brady held her in thrall with threats of, and actual, violence. This hopeless loyalty remained when both were on remand and Myra, at the request of and instructed by Brady, wrote some awful coded "sustenance" letters, very damning to her. He then, as she told me, used these letters to blackmail Myra, demanding she keep quiet about his threats to and abuse of her.

◊

Retreat from prison life

To the extent that it is possible in a closed institution, Myra tried to retreat, as much as she could, from the racket and the tumult of the prison and she surrounded herself with things that presented some form of tranquillity for her: pictures she put on the wall in her cell and the music she listened to. She loved the sound of a fountain outside at Cookham Wood Prison that she could hear from her cell, and she missed this when she moved to HMP Durham. Although, on the 7 April 1995, after recently moving there, she wrote this:

> "I've only just put the light on — the sunset sky is beautiful, looking like seas full of islands with mountains behind, and the cathedral etched against a perfect background. The birdsong is beautiful too, and the constant pealing of the bells, heard so clearly and loudly is absolutely lovely…

> …[I]t drives some people bananas but I've always loved the sound of church bells. I'm reminded, listening to them, of when I was a kid and haunted Gorton library, going almost every day because I loved the smell of the books and the rule of silence, and when I came out I sat on the low wall in front of the library which was across the road from the Church of St. James, a C of E church school that Maureen, my sister, went to when she left our primary school, and listen to the bells pealing. Haven't remembered those magic hours for centuries."

At some point, I had borrowed a psychology workbook and one of the questions in it was something along the lines of, "How would you describe yourself" personality-wise? The answers were multiple choice; I cannot remember the other three options, but the one she picked was to my astonishment "happy-go-lucky." Her answer was probably not so strange as it seemed, as I do feel this was the blueprint of her personality: light-hearted, and easy going. She was caring and liked children and animals. This had nothing to do with an act being put on or with pretence; she genuinely loved them. In prison, she became godmother to quite a few children of various friends. She had the tendency to mother and fuss over me.

◊

Owning-up and showing remorse

One of the many things Myra was criticised for was that she never owned up to her crimes or never showed remorse or not enough remorse. But she did. And when she did, her words of penitence, atonement, reparation, private anguish or guilt would be flung back at her; it would be said that she did not mean it, or that she was just saying it to get parole or our sympathy. Damned if she does, and damned if she doesn't.

In 1976 when in Holloway Prison, she won the Koestler Awards scheme[1] competition singing two Joan Baez songs (*Prison Trilogy* and *Love Song to a Stranger*) and a Tim Hardin song (*Don't Make Promises*).

One of the award judges said that he had found them "gentle, quite compelling and with a strange beauty," and *Love Song to a Stranger* was "the best solo I have heard in my four years of judging." Later, in 1996, in a letter of June 21 Myra explained:

> "David [Astor, former editor of *The Observer*] helped Arthur Koestler to set that up, after Koestler had escaped to England after being imprisoned by fascists, and wrote articles for the 'Observer'. I met Koestler long before I knew David, when he came to D wing in Holloway to talk to a group of us. Such a sad man. He committed suicide—not because of coming to Holloway, I hope."

In Cookham Wood Prison, she obtained her BA Humanities degree, in the Arts Faculty of the Open University (1980). Again, these hard won achievements were immediately interpreted as her manipulating the authorities to get parole. Myra was quoted as saying, "After all, what will it matter to the decision-makers that I've obtained a degree, when I wasn't sent to prison because I was illiterate?"

Her Open University enrolment had been discussed at Ministerial level and it was at this point that Myra realised she was being treated as a special case, and it was this that prompted the somewhat bizarre 'escape plot'[2] (see *Timeline*).

Below I give a few examples of Myra trying to express her deep regret. Apart from her article in *The Guardian* (18 December 1995), where she explained why she found it difficult to show remorse publicly, one reason she had not shown any repentance earlier in public can be found in a fragment of a letter from her:

---

1. See koestlertrust.org.uk
2. During the early 1970s Myra formed an intense friendship with a prison officer, Patricia Cairns, who before joining HM Prison Service had been a Carmelite nun. They initiated a plan to "spring" Myra and to then flee to Brazil and work as missionaries there. The "escape plot" was foiled, and, at the Old Bailey, Cairns received a six year prison sentence, and Myra an additional 12 months to run concurrently with her existing sentences.

"I have this awful confusing theory that because I deserve to suffer I should keep it all within me and not offer it up ..."

The following is an extract from a letter from her correspondence with the British film censor John Trevelyan in September 1974:

"'[G]iving up' That's just how I feel at the moment. Something is slowly dying inside me, and it's the will to live. Although I more than subscribe to Nietzche's 'he who has the why to live can be with almost any how', at the same time I feel like the prisoner whom Frankl talks about, when he said, 'Woe to him who sees no more sense in his life, no aim, no purpose, and therefore, no point in carrying on ... He is soon lost.' I don't know if it is acute depression which makes me feel deep in my heart, that I'll never be released, or if so, not until I'm quite old. I feel tortured with grief and remorse about the disaster I have caused others and I can hardly live myself. I feel I just want to drag myself into a corner, in the dark, as does an animal when it knows it is dying, and if I had no moral responsibilities and didn't owe so much to so many people, I think I could quite easily do so now."

And in a written statement by her, published in the *Guardian* in April 1974:

"There are many things in my past of which I'm deeply and bitterly ashamed, things which have bitten deeply into the inmost depths of my soul, leaving wounds which gaped agonisingly for many years before they healed into scars which I will bear for the rest of my life ..."

Also from a written statement in the public domain January 1997:

"Regarding the nature of the crimes in which I was involved, nobody but myself can be fully aware of their heinousness ... what I was involved in is etched into my heart and mind, and my conscience will follow me to my dying day ...

> In addition to the crimes themselves, I have been the cause of the suffering and anguish of the parents and relatives of the victims, and my own family and friends too. I have said before that if I could turn back the clock, I would be desperate to do so. If I could undo what I have done, I would be desperate to do so. I have done all that is in my power to make amends, but I know this is no consolation to the victims' families. It will not take away their pain and suffering."

◊

In a letter to me Myra (harking back and referring to the situation she now found herself in) writes the following (5 June 1996):

> "That's what struck a chord; emotional blackmail, feelings of guilt—if I hadn't done this, her [Myra's mother's] life would have been different; the voice of common sense says sure it would, but it could have been as bad in different ways. When my sister died, I tormented myself—not deliberately—with thoughts that if she hadn't had the rotten life she had with that bastard Smith, made worse by the crimes I committed with Brady, maybe she wouldn't have had a brain haemorrhage and died after probably the seven happiest years of her life with Bill, and five of them with Sharon [Myra's niece]...but still I was riddled with guilt. Until dear, wise John Trevelyan, to whom I'd written and had poured out my heart to, for he'd been like a father to me, wrote and told me that life, the life I'd written to him about wasn't a Greek tragedy where the gods took revenge on one who had 'sinned' by punishing, with death or sorrow, the ones who were loved and cherished by the 'sinner'. Good grief, how did I get off on this tangent? I know, I must write to my mother today. (smile)"

◊

Meeting another woman serial killer

Why hasn't Rosemary West taken Myra's place? Why not the same media/press public opinion-based obsession with her? Rosemary was convicted of ten counts of murder, but Mae and Stephen West's book apart there has been no truly serious attempt to use the "monster" label or to demonise her in quite the same way as occurred with Myra.[3] If, however, Rose West's active participation in ten killings with the sexual degradation allegedly involving her husband Fred were to be believed, it is clear that her acts were worse than Myra's. Maybe some way of explaining this absence of demonisation is:

1. I think there could be a question of residual guilt, i.e. despite social services having had a litany of complaints about the treatment of the West's children, and despite the fact that several of those children subsequently vanished, nothing was done.
2. Number 25 Cromwell Street was possibly at the centre of an organized abuse network. Debbie Cameron: "It was also rumoured (and several reporters claiming 'inside information' assured me the rumours were true) that the authorities were covering-up, or at least refusing to fully investigate, the true extent of the abuse that went on in the "House of Horrors," in which many people besides the Wests—including police officers—may have been involved." (*Trouble & Strife*, 34, p.45)
3. Rose West's active participation already sets her apart from the rest of us, so there is no *need* to demonise her. She is no threat because we *know* we are not like her.
4. And of course, when putting Myra's and Rose West's mugshots next to each other, Rose is just not good monster-type casting!

I have met Rose in person. This was in Durham Prison. After her conviction she was in the health care centre for a while, routinely placed

---

3. See *Inside 25 Cromwell Street: The Terrifying and True Story of Life with Fred and Rose West*, Peter Grose Ltd, 1995. For an account of the Cromwell Street murders, see, e.g. *The Cromwell Street Murders: The Detective's Story*, Bennett, J, The History Press, 2006.

on suicide watch. One day, Myra (who was also there at the time) suggested inviting Rose for a cup of tea; so we did.

I could not empathise with Rose, whereas with Myra, as will have been evident from what I have said already, quite the opposite was true; on the whole, people who knew Myra liked her.

Free-spirited Myra compared

One thing I noticed was that Myra was such a free spirit, she was open-minded and interested in new things, different things. The fact that I am from Holland was, for example, a new source of interest for her and she asked me if I could teach her Dutch. Other prisoners would quite soon get institutionalised. I did not feel that with Myra. Practical new things naturally surprised her; she told me when she first came across sliding doors at the hospital she was amazed by them. I once asked her how she managed to cope with all these endless years of incarceration. She answered: "Auto-pilot."

Reflecting on the person I knew, I now wonder if her answer quite covers the essence. For if this were true, I think she too *would* have been institutionalised. I believe she had found an inner resourcefulness that had helped her through the decades of drudgery, and her enormous resilience being, of course, another important factor. She refers to this in the following extract:

> "I've got myself together again after months of complete hell. I thought for a time that I'd be unable to do so, for I don't think I've ever felt so utterly low and helpless in my entire life before, but I guess resilience is part of my make-up (an adjective someone else applied to me many months ago, and not for the first time either). I've often hated myself before but this time I hated myself so much, I could hardly live with myself. I still haven't completely purged all the hate away, but enough of it to have been able to partly come to terms with myself and life. I can't attribute that to time, for unfortunately, time sometimes stands still; it must be the urge for self-preservation. During that prolonged period, I often used to think of steel,

> in order to derive inspiration or whatever. I'm glad I read up the processing of it, for I remembered all the stages it had to go through before all the impurities and everything were eradicated. I must be one of those pieces which have to keep going back into the furnace, and I certainly leapt in there myself this time. (smile)" [4]

Although Myra was not institutionalised in the way that some prisoners are, increasingly over-reliant on things being done for them, I did sometimes sense an inertia. For example, when she wrote the article for *The Guardian* she found it an effort to keep working at it; I thought, however, it was important that *her* voice was heard instead of these "debates" about her which were not getting anywhere, such as on *Panorama* or *Heart of the Matter*, "Can We Forgive Myra Hindley?" (as if this was some prerequisite for her release). Seldom were these programmes solely about the merits of her case, that is, was she being treated differently to other lifers? Had her case become a political one? To "balance" such programmes the relatives of the victims were always invited; and as their comments were naturally often emotive and therefore unarguable the discussion regarding her case never really moved forward. All that happened was the recreating of public outrage at the crimes.

4. From a letter to Joanna Kozubska reproduced in *Cries for Help: Women Without a Voice, Women's Prisons in the 1970s, Myra Hindley and her Contemporaries*, Waterside Press, 2014, p. 138.

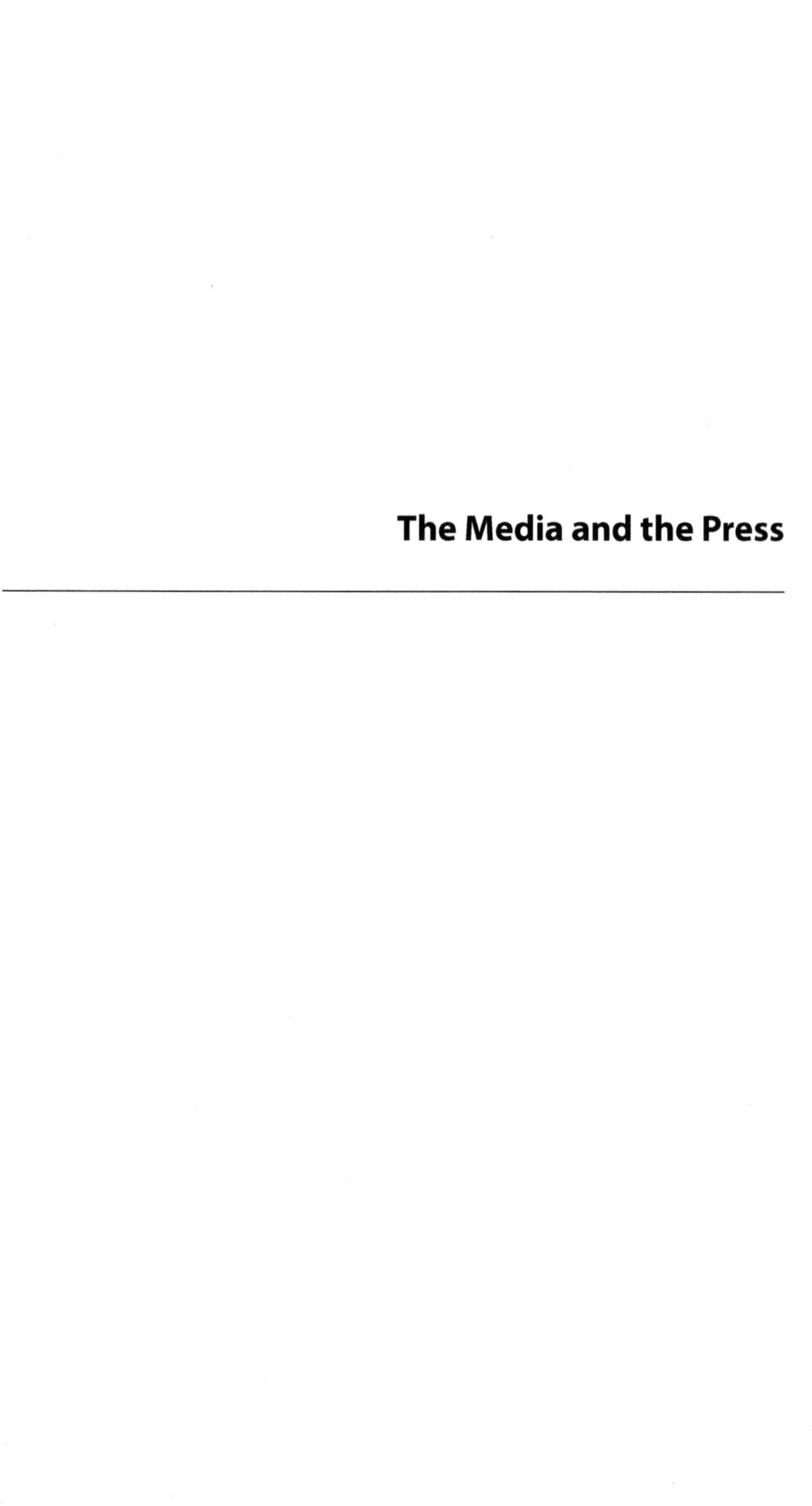

The Media and the Press

"You can't be an outsider and be successful over 30 years without leaving a certain amount of scar tissue around the place."

Rupert Murdoch

"I hate journalists. There is nothing in them but tittering jeering emptiness ... The shallowest people on the ridge of the earth."

W B Yeats

"The chief thing is to have a soul that loves the truth and harbours it where it finds it. And another thing: the truth requires constant repetition because error is being preached about us all the time, and not only by isolated individuals but by the masses. In newspapers and encyclopaedias, in schools and universities, everywhere error rides high and basks in the consciousness of having the majority on its side."

Goethe

"Assemble a mob of men and women previously conditioned by a daily reading of newspapers; treat them to amplified band music, bright lights, and the oratory of a demagogue who ... is simultaneously the exploiter and the victim of herd-intoxication, and in next to no time you can reduce them to a state of almost mindless subhumanity. Never before have so few been in a position to make fools, maniacs or criminals, of so many."

Aldous Huxley, *The Devils of Loudun*, 1952

CHAPTER 6

The Media and the Press

Strictly speaking the media and press are expected to observe certain standards. The following are just some of the provisions of the Press Standards Organization Code of Practice.

Code of Practice

1. Accuracy

(i) Newspapers and periodicals should take care not to publish inaccurate, misleading or distorted material including pictures.

(ii) Whenever it is recognised that a significant inaccuracy, misleading statement or distorted report has been published, it should be corrected promptly and with due prominence.

(iii) An apology must be published whenever appropriate.

(iv) Newspapers, whilst free to be partisan, must distinguish clearly between comment, conjecture and fact.

(v) A newspaper or periodical must report fairly and accurately the outcome of an action for defamation to which it has been party.

3. Privacy

(i) Everyone is entitled to respect for his or her private and family life, home, health and correspondence. A publication will be expected to justify intrusions into any individual's private life without consent.

(ii) The use of long lens photography to take pictures of people in private places without their consent is unacceptable.

4. Harassment

(i) Journalists and photographers must neither obtain nor seek to obtain information or pictures through intimidation, harassment or persistent pursuit.

(ii) They must not photograph individuals in private places[1] without their consent; must not persist in telephoning, questioning, pursuing or photographing individuals after having been asked to desist; must not remain on their property after having been asked to leave and must not follow them.

(iii) Editors must ensure that those working for them comply with these requirements and must not publish material from other sources which does not meet these requirements.

The need for some kind of regulation goes back a long way and is embedded in the nature and culture of newspaper publishing, especially in relation to the tabloids.

> "At the start of the 20th-century Edwardian press barons were demanding a murder a day for the pleasure of their readers." Historian and TV presenter Dr Lucy Worsley in "A Very British Murder" (BBC4) (18 September 2013).

The Tyburn broadsheets were similar to the tabloid press of nowadays. Tens of thousands of people would flock to Tyburn (the London place of execution from 1196–1783; on the site of the modern-day Marble Arch) to watch a hanging (or several): in the late 1700s one could be hanged for offences such as stealing from a rabbit warren, cutting down a young tree, or being in the company of gypsies for a month. People would be doing a roaring trade selling food and drink. Pamphlets (known as broadsheets) were sold with all kinds of juicy stories about murders, witchcraft and of course about the crime committed by those being executed, and very often the creators of these would use their imagination to embellish the crime, much the same as what happens with the tabloids of today. In that respect, not a lot has changed in, say, 500 years. As it was then,

1. As defined by a note to Clause 3.

it is now; crime is part of amusement, the news is not just for business but also for entertainment. In the end result and final analysis newspapers must sell their coverage and stories (or with free newspapers attract advertisers) in order to survive. Whatever, the battle is primarily to book circulation and any objective look at the everyday "news" and headlines shows how these are packaged to that end.

There were to be sure some particularly courageous journalists who spoke out on Myra's behalf and who expressed their distaste of her treatment by the press and the state. For example and to identify a few, the following all showed support through their writing:

- Simon Jenkins, journalist and editor, said that Myra's treatment was not worthy of a Western European civilised society, but more akin to that of a banana republic;
- Richard Ingrams: "... Myra Hindley ... would have been released long ago without much fuss had it not been for the press." (*The Observer*, 11 December 1994);
- Suzanne Moore: "There is of course more than one way of taking a life and we have taken Hindley's." ("Are you just one of Myra's lynch mob?," *The Independent*, 7 February 1997);
- Germaine Greer: "Even hard-boiled journalists write nonsense about her, apparently unaware that her compellingness is their own creation." ("Revengers Tragedy," *The Guardian*, 20 December 1994).

◊

Myra as an engineered national obsession

There is perhaps no nation so obsessed and fascinated by crime as the British. In the early-1960s, Myra Hindley was an accomplice to someone else's crimes and the trial judge, Mr Justice Fenton Atkinson, saw her as being redeemable. The general understanding was she would be released at some point. Even according to the *Sun* whose inside leader on 14 September 1972 read: "Prison is for reform as well as punishment and it may be true she is no longer a menace. Perhaps one day she should go free." (How times changed!) In 1985 she was judged fit for parole yet by 1994 she was "the most evil woman in the world" (and Michael Howard drew up his list of murderers who, for "public acceptability" reasons, would never be released: see *Chapter 4*). Although she was again considered fit for parole in 1996, in 1997 she had become a "serial killer," the "most hated woman in Britain," and the "embodiment of evil"; and, according to the Home Office, her crimes had become so "heinous" she could never be released. What had happened?

In 1969 an Australian businessman, Rupert Murdoch, became the "new kid on the block" when he bought an ailing British broadsheet called *The Sun*. This started off a ruthless tabloid newspaper war, and Myra Hindley's fate was sealed. With the help of a terrible mugshot, which kept on being recycled in spite of other photos being available, Myra was slowly created into a monster "who slaughtered and tortured innocent tots."

She explained to me how this dreadful picture had come into being. She was led into a room, and thought she was going to be interrogated in a rather heavy-handed way. The moment she braced herself for what she feared was coming, the light bulb of the camera flashed, and the iconic photo was created. The unrelenting and vitriolic crusade the tabloids embarked on was in its intensity and ferocity unparalleled in media and English penal history; it was the most concentrated campaign ever conducted in print against an individual, with the (successful) aim of preventing her gaining parole.[2]

---

2. Quite the reverse occurred in the case of Private Lee Clegg. Clegg was sentenced in 1993 to life imprisonment for his involvement in the killing of two teenage joyriders, 18-year-old Karen Reilly and the 17-year-old driver, Martin Peake. The joyriders drove through an army checkpoint in West Belfast. A large number of shots were fired by the soldiers, Clegg firing four of them, the last bullet going through the back of the car when it was leaving and therefore no longer a threat. The tabloids, spearheaded by the *Daily Mail*, launched a campaign to have Clegg's conviction overturned. His parents were interviewed on *This Morning* (24 January 1995). Apparently, it had initially been intended to include the parents of Karen Reilly in the programme, to present the opposing view, but their appearance was cancelled at the last moment. They also ran a telephone poll where viewers could respond to the question: "Should Private Lee Clegg be released immediately?" Only one telephone number was given, though. In other words, you could only vote "yes." Relatives and friends of Karen who rang the number to protest at the programme's lack of balance were horrified to find out that they had voted for Clegg's immediate release. He was released after four years in prison, resumed his career in the Army and was promoted to sergeant.

Every reported move she made in prison was portrayed as evidence of her "evilness." The tabloids were aided and abetted by Brady, who would, whenever he saw an occasion, try to damn Myra by saying she was as culpable as he was. And the tabloids would regard the rants of this man, who for many years has been diagnosed as insane, to be reliable denouncements.

It was even suggested that Myra enjoyed the publicity! She was also blamed for always seeking publicity. I think it was around ten times in 36 years that she in fact approached the media. Another reason for the sheer volume of "Myra" stories was that they sold papers. Any tabloid editor could have told you that he could guarantee sales by putting one of two women on the front page: the other was Her Royal Highness Diana, Princess of Wales.

The satirical radio current affairs sketch programme *Week Ending*, Radio Four, on 29 September 1995 asked:

> "Did you see that picture of Myra Hindley on a pony? She's supposed to be in prison, not the bleeding circus. *The Sun* ought to run a story every day telling us to forget Myra Hindley and let the relatives grieve in peace."

Many of the *Sun's* "exclusives" regarding Myra Hindley have had the by-line of its now ex-"chief reporter," John Kay. In 1977, Kay drowned his Japanese wife, Harue, in the bath, and then attempted to kill himself several times. He was convicted of manslaughter on the grounds of diminished responsibility, and ordered to be admitted for treatment in a psychiatric hospital in North London. After his stay in Friern Barnet Hospital, Kay was welcomed back by the *Sun*.[3] Could what we have been reading in the numerous articles about Myra be, in fact, his sense of guilt projected onto her? A form of scapegoating.

> "In so far as the process is unconscious, it is more likely to be denied by the perpetrator. In such cases, any bad feelings—such as the perpetrator's own shame and guilt—are also likely to be denied…Scapegoating frees the

3. This information from *Stick it Up Your Punter! The Rise and Fall of the Sun*, Peter Chippendale and Chris Horrie, Heinemann, 1990.

> perpetrator from some self-dissatisfaction and provides some narcissistic gratification to him. It enables the self-righteous discharge of aggression" (Kraup-Taylor 1953).

Myra's perpetual incarceration and lack of privileges she had earned in the near to four decades of her sentence were determined almost totally by Rupert Murdoch and Lord Rothermere (*Daily Mail*). No wonder Myra loved Dennis Potter (the screenwriter and dramatist) for calling his cancer Rupert.

Even television news and programmes such as BBC 2's *Newsnight* do not always manage to get their facts right. A previous employee of the BBC once told me that the researchers are too young to remember the case, so they rely on whatever has been written since, and this can also mean acquiring "facts" from reading back-copies of *The Sun*. Hence *Newsnight* anchor Jeremy Paxman introducing one lead item by saying: "Myra Hindley, the woman who (*with her lover*) tortured and murdered five children ... " moreover "*the woman raised to become the embodiment of human evil* will never be released" (27 January 1997).

I once sent an article I had written to a journalist who was working at the time for the *Independent on Sunday*; he embellished it with an "interview" with me. Consequently, much of the article that appeared in the paper was not in my words nor in my style; not to mention the awful made-up tabloidy headline "How I fell in love with Myra."

Whilst the tabloids have casually described me as an ex-con/ex-prisoner, in *The Daily Telegraph* it was once claimed I was studying to become a contemplative nun! Of course, neither is true. And so the tabloids chase the illusion they have created.

When the Press Complaints Commission upheld a complaint Myra made against *The Daily Mail*, who had claimed that she and Rose West had a "special relationship," *BBC News* invited me to be interviewed on her behalf. Sure enough, not long afterwards, *The Daily Mail* "doorstepped" me and as a result I was kept holed-up in my flat for a couple of days and had to crawl along the floor to keep away from a long lens camera. After they left they went to Holland to harass my mother and God knows who else; and on their return produced a vindictive and defamatory article about me containing untruths, half-truths and inaccuracies.

Kevin Toolis wrote an interesting article in *The Guardian* (*Guardian Weekend*, 9 November 1996) about the tabloid procedure. He described how he, together with a photographer, doorstepped a teacher to "monster" him (the verb "to monster" was apparently coined by tabloid feature writers).The "crime" of the teacher was banning a fashion show at his school. They turned up unannounced on his doorstep, and, "[I]t did not matter what [the subject] said or did, as far as my editors were concerned, he was guilty... We needed a picture." Which they duly took without consent. Tabloid stories have less impact without a photograph, the more devious looking the better.

One evening as I was watching *Newsnight,* Jeremy Paxman picked up the next morning's papers and read out *The Sun* headlines. I thus learnt I had married Myra; I nearly fell off my chair. This story was later retracted by *The Sun*, but only partly, because no mention was made of the untruthfulness of the article. The retraction consisted of only two sentences including: "... We have been asked to make it clear, and are happy to do so, that Father Bert White was not present and played no part in any such event" (22 August 1995). Bert White was the prison chaplain at Cookham Wood Prison; in 1999, when he was staying at a presbytery, he sadly died in a freak accident caused by the fumes of a faulty television when it caught fire. Myra was devastated by his death.

Pavlov's dog

The relentlessness of the tabloids created a Pavlov's dog-like reaction in people in relation to Myra Hindley and somewhere a residual of her as projected even appeared to have rubbed off on me. For example, when I went to visit her at Highpoint Prison, it sometimes happened, when I passed a section of the prison, that inmates would bang on the windows with such vehemence that I thought the glass would break. Visitors would threaten me and swear at me. Privacy laws work in other countries, and people's names do not tend to get dragged through the mud.

One day I walked down Holloway Road when I bumped into an ex-inmate from Cookham Wood. I had got to know her a little, and I remember sitting in the prison garden reading Oscar Wilde's *The Ballad of Reading Gaol* to her. Suffering from delirium tremens, she initially spent some time in the sick bay, where Myra, for health and safety reasons, was also staying; there were never any problems between the two of them. So it was nice to see her, but it was obvious she had been drinking again. She approached me with a smile; then, for a moment, I saw confusion in her eyes before she started screaming at me with fury; it became clear she had associated me with Myra and "Monster Myra" from the media had usurped the person she knew from sick bay.

The misconceptions that circulated about Myra's case amongst the general public and even amongst some MPs were due to a barrage of "evil-Myra" tabloid stories sustained over decades—in nearly every *The Sun* article about her, her name is prefixed or attached to the word "evil"—I only have to look at the fictitious articles about her and myself to understand how powerful the written word is.

The ritualised and repetitive campaign that was based on myths rather than reality became so entrenched that people just stopped thinking about it and simply accepted it as being "true," and with that, the belief that the crimes she had committed were worse and more hateful than those ever committed by anyone else.

All criminal lawyers know that Myra Hindley's offences were not unique, so do the regular readers of our newspapers and so would anyone who would care to look at the events in which she was involved. With the enormous help of the media, the nation has been made to remember, more often misremember, and even invent her offences. Her crimes had ballooned *so* out of proportion that her name got casually bracketed with the likes of Hitler, Pol Pot and Saddam Hussein. Blake Morrison in the *Weekend Guardian* of 1 February 1997 wrote "... It doesn't make them [the juvenile killers Thompson and Venables[4]] 'freaks of nature'

4. Ten-year-old Robert Thompson and Jon Venables were convicted of the murder of two-year-old James Bulger. Blake Morrison, in his book, *As If* on the case wrote: "The pre-publicity has been prejudicial, they say: the emotive language and saturation coverage can't help but have influenced the jury. David Turner, defending them, has assembled 147 press cuttings, which compare the accused to Myra Hindley and Saddam Hussein."

nor comparable to Myra Hindley or Saddam Hussein." Michael Buerk on BBC Radio Four's *The Moral Maze*, 31 July 1997, asked, "How do we explain evil on the level of Pol Pot, or Myra Hindley?" and on the Jimmy Young radio show of 1 March 1985, Tom Pendry MP apparently said:

> "[The 'Moors murders' were] so horrifying that the Nuremberg trials pale into insignificance by comparison, in many ways."

Anything goes, anyone can say anything about Myra, or could threaten her with impunity. I once read that from a psychological point of view every society needs its "demons," that is, those hate-figures representing the human unconscious, figures on whom people can project their own feelings of fear and inadequacy. It was George Orwell who in his novel *1984* illustrated how the state influences and controls people by inventing the safety valve of the regimented and routine "two minutes hate" when citizens could down tools and were expected to pour venom at an image projected on a large communal screen. The country has, with unrelenting help from the tabloids over the past decades, turned Myra Hindley into such a monster. An icon of evil is a great comfort to society.

The fact that she was the accomplice and not the instigator or the perpetrator of the offences (as already emphasised) was, with considerable help from the tabloids, forgotten by most people. She has been regularly and routinely portrayed as the main offender "who committed these crimes with her lover Ian Brady."

BBC TV Ceefax: "... and Brady as her 'accomplice killer.'" Brady had virtually disappeared. Their joint enterprise had become, "Myra Hindley's Moors Murders," and *his* victims indisputably *hers*. They were even dubbed the "Hindley crimes," this by one psychologist I seem to recall. On 29 November 1997 according to Teletext:

> "Murder victims' relatives march on Downing Street, demanding that life should mean life... Dozens of families who have lost their loved ones to killers such as Myra Hindley and Frederick West."

A doomed attempt to retrieve matters

> Psychopathy is probably about as common in women as it is in men. However its manifestations are different, with the lack of empathy tending to be of a more spiteful and less physically violent nature in psychopathic women than men. Even when they engage in targeted aggression, female psychopaths are much less likely to do so using physical violence than are their male counterparts. Quite simply, their body structure and sexual biology are not adapted for it. There are rare documented cases of women engaged in violent crime, such as the infamous moors murderess Myra Hindley, and Rosemary West; but in both these cases and many others the driving force was a dominating CNE[5]/psychopathic male. In the absence of the dominant male it is highly improbable that these violent crimes would have occurred at all.[6]

On a few occasions it had been suggested that Myra was a psychopath. So, when the *Guardian* printed an edited extract from the book *A Mind to Crime* by Anne Moir and David Jessel, in which Myra was labelled as such, she responded to it by sending a letter to the newspaper. The following is an excerpt from it (4 October 1995):

> "I couldn't believe my eyes when I picked up my Guardian on Saturday to see at the top of the front page a 30-year-old police mugshot of myself beside a heading: 'Can criminals be diagnosed and cured?' I thought for a moment I'd been given the Sun by mistake. And when I turned to Weekend Guardian and read the edited extract from 'A mind to crime' by Anne Moir and David Jessel, with a photograph of myself aged eight alongside that awful mugshot again, I couldn't believe what I was seeing and reading…

> The female psychopath is four times rarer than the male and there is a suggestion that women psychopaths appear to seek out their male equivalents to commit their crimes. Psychopathy baffles us because it is a mental

5. Constitutional negative empath.
6. David P Anderson and Nigel C Scott, *Three False Convictions, Many Lessons: The Psychopathology of Unjust Prosecutions,* Waterside Press (2016).

> disease that wears the mask of sanity. Sufferers feel justified in their actions, however horrific.
>
> To be casually labelled a psychopath by two people who have never met or spoken to me flies in the face of reason. In my 30 years in prison I have met, spoken with and been examined by psychiatrists and, in particular, a senior psychologist with whom I did a series of tests, the results of which ruled out psychopathy, schizophrenia, manic depression, episodic dyscontrol and any form of psychosis or neurosis. In a word, there was no evidence of a mentally disordered mind. And my EEGs revealed no abnormalities or dysfunctions ..."

The Guardian then asked Myra if she could justify her letter and invited her to write an article for them to explain what then had made her commit these horrific crimes.

I would have thought that a self-analytical piece written by her would be something that the public had been waiting for years. But this was not the reaction of the Home Office or later letters written to *The Guardian*. How *dare* it give her a platform? It seemed that any explanation as to *why* she got involved in these horrendous crimes was of no interest. Myra wrote to me once:

> "I also believe I'm hated not just because I'm feared, but because people fear that they could have been me, given the type of person I was after I met Brady, and given the circumstances. It's true that we hate what we fear, and what we fear we reject."

Most people were not even born when the crimes happened. Myra:

> "[T]hey hadn't had the chance to form their own independent 'judgement', and by the time they were old enough to do so, they couldn't express their opinion for fear of bringing down the wrath of their parents and parents' contemporaries."

Myra did not only get criticised for trying to explain how she got involved in the crimes but also for the reasoned way she expressed herself. When she "officially" confessed in 1987, Helena Kennedy in *Eve Was Framed*[7] suggested,

> "The lucid explanation that Myra Hindley herself puts forward to explain (but not excuse) her involvement in the killings — that she was a naïve young girl totally in the thrall of a complex and experienced man — misses its mark because of the very coherence with which it is expressed. From the knowledge of her as she is now, the public find it very hard to extract a sense of the woman she was then."

Similarly, in her article "Are you just one of Myra's lynch mob?" Suzanne Moore said, "As time goes by she becomes increasingly articulate and we understand her less and less, condemn her more and more." (*Independent*, 7 February 1997). People do change; and the many years of imprisonment had given Myra plenty of opportunity for introspection and repentance. And that she could articulate herself well, should be taken as a positive, as indeed it normally would be. But not so in Myra Hindley's case. In a *Sunday Times* article (18 December 1994), Lesley White stated that Hindley "deconstructs her plight like a trained sociologist."

More ostracising, and strange imaginings

Myra once told me that the police visited her friend May, as they did with practically everyone who knew Myra as a child and teenager. May told the police how Myra had confided in her that she was afraid of Brady; that he had drugged her, and that Myra had given her a letter to take to the police if she, Myra, disappeared. She described Myra as perfectly normal until she met Brady. This friend was later ostracised and vilified for what people thought of as "helping Myra." Although Myra later

7. Vintage edn., 1993, p.247.

either asked her to destroy or return the letter, it nevertheless clearly shows that she was, for a time at least, terrified of Brady before actually becoming an extension of him.

I do not in any way want to downplay her part in the crimes, they were appalling, but I *do* think that the way her role in them has been used has been a convenience for so many of us in so many ways. Myra became a commodity for numerous people to use for their own ends and needs. She described herself as a lucky-dip box with everyone dipping in for parts of her. It was not just that people projected *on her what* they *did not* want her to be, that is, human, there were also those who projected onto her what they *wanted* her to be: she received letters from individuals who thought she was their mother, there were strangers who were in love with her, wanted to marry her, and so forth.

Myra As Public Property

"One of the many lessons that one learns in prison is, that things are what they are and will be what they will be."

Oscar Wilde

CHAPTER 7

Myra As Public Property

Myra had become public property. Some prison officers did not even dare to talk too long with her, out of fear that someone might comment on it. Myra:

> "The general consensus appears to be that I am a piece of public property, with most people having their own perceptions and opinions of me, and far too many people saying what I should or shouldn't do. I have never subscribed to or identified with these distorted perceptions and misrepresentations of myself, striving always to retain my identity and individuality in a system which, it could cynically be said, seems to strip them from one along with one's clothes upon reception …
>
> I often think of a lifer as a caged budgie. Many years ago in Holloway, when a budgie escaped from a small aviary and fluttered up onto the high perimeter wall, it hesitated, hearing the cries of the inmates trying to coax it down, then it spread its wings and soared over the wall into a tree, where it flew from branch to branch before disappearing from sight. We all knew the budgie probably wouldn't survive for very long if it remained free, but unlike the bird a lifer is aware of what can be described as the hazards of freedom and can take them on board." (Extract from *Verdict, The Magazine of the Oxford University Law Society,* Hilary, 1996).

Bees around the honey pot

I gradually became aware that people were often quite obsessed with Myra and would not let her go. Father Bert White (mentioned earlier) used to call these people bees around the honey pot. Myra herself once compared it to a boat; so many people had made their way onto her boat that it was in danger of sinking. She also once wrote to me describing herself as a heavy pollen-overloaded flower attracting millions of bees, all busy following their very own personal agenda. They felt they had to make Myra their business, and had an opinion about her and her every move; and some people would turn against her if they thought she was not giving them enough of her time and attention.

Bruised egos

An example of the honeypot syndrome or "owning Myra" was when Myra decided to try and take more control of her own life. When she received her whole life tariff she concluded she did not need one particular official contact anymore. This individual, who seemingly did not want to let go of such a high-profile inmate and also apparently believed she was the only one who could deal with such "a politically sensitive prisoner," appeared to be determined to put in a personal, negative report on Myra. What she tried to achieve "fell through" though, and her comments stood out like a sore thumb amongst the other reports which the Parole Board is bound to consider. She was not the only example, though. There was also a prison officer/counsellor who visited Cookham Wood. He was at first helpful and sympathetic to Myra but became, in my view, unethical, possibly vindictive. After the counselling had finished and shortly after Myra had been transferred to Durham, the counsellor wanted to visit her. Prisoners, however, get only a certain number of visiting orders, and Myra wanted to use hers on me and not on him. He was unhappy about this, and I think it would be fair to say that his subsequent contributions to the discussion about Myra should be seen in this light; as it appeared, he found it difficult to hide his disappointment whenever speaking (publicly) about her. For example, regarding a television programme about Myra, on which this counsellor appeared, Myra's old priest commented in a letter (1997) to her that he "... was dismayed by [the counsellor's] actions, but, in all honesty, wasn't too surprised;" and he said further that "it seemed he was overstepping the mark in betraying confidences." Indeed, to say the least, his notion of client confidentiality was rather unorthodox. Arguably, these people exploited their professional or other standing to punish someone dependent on them and so far as I can see for no other reason then their bruised egos.

But there were also champions ...

Yet Myra did have a good many supporters even if as described in *Chapter 10* most of them were not prepared to come out into the open. One of Myra's old assistant governors from Holloway Prison always stayed in touch with her. She helped Myra to get started on her education; she coached her for her German O-Level, which Myra did by correspondence course. She once mentioned to me that she felt some people were addicted to Myra. What this governor remembered about Myra was that she got on well with people, was very sociable and likeable, definitely not an outsider; she found her intelligent and always thought that if her circumstances (her background) had been different she would have gone a long way in life.

Noticeably, Myra attracted some eminent champions over the years. Although her supporters naturally just wanted to act in her best interest they did sometimes tend to behave in a way regarding Myra as *they* saw best, ignoring her wishes or choices and often making decisions for her. It appeared that some people preferred her to stand still, and for *them* to lead *her* life for her, on *their* terms. Other people noticed this too; Myra mentioned to me that a television producer, who was making a programme about her case at the time, likened Myra to her disabled sister in a wheelchair; she said the family and everyone just talked over her head as if she wasn't there. The good intentions of her supporters were occasionally felt to be stifling by Myra, and she tried to prevent them, as she described it, "from erecting more bars around [her] … If I adhered to their every wish and advice, I'd be in a tiny bird cage."

Then there was also the disastrous, if well-meaning, intervention of Lord Longford, courting publicity in all the wrong ways. Frank Longford (1905–2001), as many people seemed to know him, was a lifelong penal reform campaigner who, in his way, tried to win parole for Myra. He was brave and right to try to achieve this, yet the way he courted publicity only resulted in damaging her case even more. They met in 1968 and for a long time he used to visit Myra but could not resist talking to the press afterwards and describing her as "a good religious woman." He could not understand and refused to listen to anyone, myself included (and this was when he was kind enough to invite me to lunch at the House of Lords), who tried to make him see his contact with the press did her case more harm than good.

Jimmy Boyle so aptly notes in his book, *The Pain of Confinement* (Pan, 1985, pp.180–181) that:

> "He knows what he is doing when he is dealing with the media and this makes it all the worse as he seems impervious to the destructive way the media use him, particularly in the way he has given Myra Hindley the 'kiss of death.'"

Myra became exasperated and felt compelled to cease receiving visits from him; although they still wrote to each other and he did very occasionally still visit her. By attending television "debates," Lord Longford gave the impression that it was perfectly acceptable for the "public" to discuss and decide the fate of individual prisoners.

The media arena is, of course, never a suitable place for such a debate. In July 1997, Myra let the relevant supporters of her case know that she didn't want anyone else but herself or her solicitor to deal with the media anymore, and firmly felt that the best way to deal with the press was by ignoring them. She knew they would never go away but they wouldn't go away in any event. All the TV programmes (some mentioned earlier in the book) that had been made all resulted in the same thing, resurrecting the past, and perpetuating the same cycle of negativity; and she didn't want anyone anymore fuelling the fire by cooperating or contributing to it. She said that, if needed, an article or letter from her or statement from her solicitor would suffice to put across her views.

If only these supporters had directed some of their time and efforts on Carole Hanson (the woman who drowned herself in the bath[1]) instead of Myra Hindley, I think it would have benefited both women.

1. See *Chapter 1.*

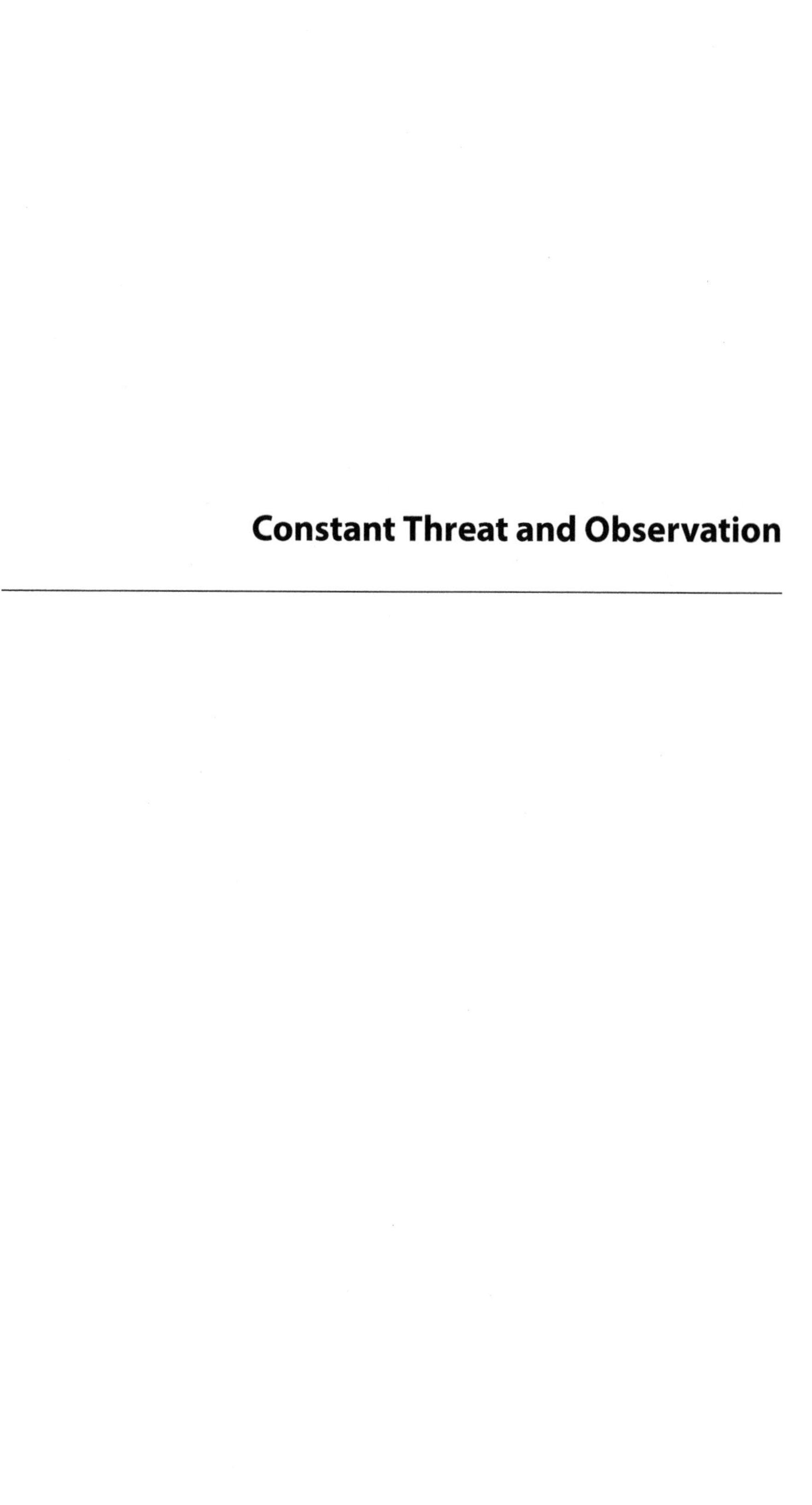

Constant Threat and Observation

"Her Majesty's Prison Service serves the public by keeping in custody those committed by the courts. Our duty is to look after them with humanity and help them lead law-abiding and useful lives in custody and after release."

HM Prison Service Mission Statement

CHAPTER 8

Constant Threat and Observation

Myra had been subjected to some brutal verbal and physical assaults. She told me she was attacked three times, twice seriously, once in Holloway Prison and twice in Cookham Wood. In Holloway in 1976, Myra was once severely and viciously beaten-up by one of the other inmates; her nose was broken, it had to be reset, she sustained a split lip and ear and two black eyes, her front teeth were loosened, and the cartilage in her knee was damaged. Yet, probably tellingly, she didn't do anything to defend herself, "But Myra did nothing. Absolutely nothing."[1]

Maybe the reluctance to defend herself is not completely surprising given that beatings were what she was used to; she abhorred violence, "... she used to shake like a leaf if she heard any trouble starting elsewhere on the wing...".[2] The first time she was assaulted in Cookham Wood was during a fight in her cell; she was attacked from behind and therefore taken by surprise, she had, amongst other injuries a lot of her hair torn out.

On 31 December 1996, Myra wrote telling me she had received relatively little "rough treatment" from staff. However:

> "There was one officer in Holloway when I first went there and had my exercise in the evening [it was late-May early-June], who always made me walk around what were called the cell-blocks, so she could revel in what was shouted out of the windows at me. But outwardly I acknowledged nothing, and she soon got bored and walked me round the gardens instead."

1. Janie Jones, *The Devil and Miss Jones: Twisted Mind of Myra Hindley* (New edn. 1994), Smith Gryphon Publishing, p.167.
2. Ibid. p.125.

She explained how the officer was briefly on the security wing where the condemned cell used to be, and that she, Myra, and a couple of other girls were trying to make a rockery. The officer opened a door that Myra hadn't noticed before and beckoned her in. It had a slab in it and a kind of chute—the officer told Myra that was where those who'd been hanged used to "fall through." Just outside was a tap where a hosepipe could be fitted, which, it was explained was used to wash away all the "muck" after they'd messed themselves at the point of death.

> "I told her I wasn't interested in her gory tales, that I was sorry, for her sake, that I hadn't been hanged...There were other nasty officers who tried to incite inmates to violence—on me—but never succeeded, and over the years I learned to treat them with the contempt they deserved and ignore their existence. But—as I've mentioned to you before—whenever I did this, they'd almost run after me asking why I wasn't speaking to them, what had they done, etc.; yuk!...
>
> I remember two officers from Holloway, who never gave the death penalty a second thought, it existed and was accepted—until they had to do 'condemned cell duty', first one of them with a Greek woman who was hanged and the other with Ruth Ellis—it horrified them and they became 'abolitionists'."

The first major "Myra story" and the first time her mugshot was used as a front page "frightener" was in the *Daily Express* concerning the fatal day in 1972 when the Governor of Holloway Prison, Mrs Dorothy Wing, took Myra out for a walk on Hampstead Heath. She routinely took prisoners, whom she knew were up for parole, out of the prison for brief trips. It was a way to acclimatise them to the world they were about to rejoin. In this case, however, the consequences of the outing were disastrous; someone informed the press about it. The press then sought confirmation from the Home Office Press Office. When this was given, some papers went "to press." Early the following morning the headlines blazoned a "public outrage" over Myra's two hours of freedom, when in fact until then the public was totally unaware. The result of the outing was that Dorothy Wing was publicly reprimanded for her act of human decency and was retired in disgrace. Myra's hope of release virtually disappeared, and last but not least, the press learnt a lucrative lesson: Myra's mugshot sold papers.[3]

Myra on 8 August 1996:

> "It is Monday morning. I hoped to finish this yesterday, but I was so heavy-eyed, I just snoozed the rest of the day away. There was an item on the news about a prisoner from Parkhurst who hoped to escape by covering his body with yellow highlighter pen so it would look as though he had jaundice, would be taken to hospital, and make his escape from there. But his plan was foiled when an officer doing a routine check looked through his inspection hatch and saw him covering his face with the pen. It reminded me of when I was on the so-called security wing in Holloway. There was an argument in the TV room about which programme should be on (there was only BBC and ITV then; a choice of two). Most of us wanted one thing, I think it was Top of the Pops, but one woman wanted to watch something on the other side. She didn't really want to watch it; she just didn't want Top of the Pops on because her 'arch enemy', a lifer friend of mine, wanted to watch it. Anyway, when the programme started, this woman got up and switched over, and someone else got up and switched it back. This went on for about 5 minutes, by which time almost everyone wanted to punch her teeth down her throat. My friend, Norma, leapt up and planted herself in front of the TV and when this pain in the ass tried to reach round her to switch over, Norma pushed her away. This woman tried to attack her with a knitting needle (she used to drive me bananas when a film or documentary was on; all I could hear was the incessant clicking of her poxy knitting needles—plastic ones hadn't been invented then, or if they had, they weren't used in prisons, only the metal ones. (Was it St Bernadette who was almost driven mad by the incessant clicking of rosary beads by another nun?), so Norma, who had a short fuse anyway, grabbed hold of her and literally threw her out of the TV room. The next morning, this woman asked to see the doctor.........Cindy, as this creature called herself, had lurid-looking

3. An extended account of the affair can be found in Joanna Kozubska's book, *Cries for Help: Myra Hindley and Her Contemporaries* (2015), Waterside Press.

> bruises on her face, neck and arms, which she said had been inflicted by Norma. Staff and inmates all knew what Cindy had done, and so did Dr Bull. With the Principal Officer present in the surgery (it was on the wing), the doctor put some cream on a large piece of cotton wool and proceeded to remove the various cosmetics Cindy had used to make her bruises. She was never able to live it down—people used to point to her eyeshadow and say 'Cindy, your eyes are bruised. Who hit you this time? etc.' Just to 'conclude this story', the same woman kept insisting she had cancer. She was taken out several times to hospital, several hospitals, and every test that was done proved that she had no cancer in her whole body. About 4 years later, and a few months before her release, she got cancer and died less than a year later. Someone said it was a classic case of wishing something upon oneself."

Although Myra did not tell me this, I know that in Holloway in 1976 she had helped to break up a fight. It happened in the wing's kitchen when a prison officer suddenly got attacked by an inmate. Myra threw herself literally between the inmate and the prison officer and because of this she got injured receiving kicks and blows that were meant for the prison officer. This prison officer expressed the wish that Myra would be properly thanked for her unselfish behaviour and that it would also be recorded in her favour.

I understand that from the early released Home Office documents about Myra, it has transpired that her presence on the wing was seen as beneficial and useful. It was said she had a calming influence.

Once when visiting Myra at Highpoint Prison, I found she had arranged to have a bag of her property handed out to me (This was because of a new rule stating that all prisoners, irrespective of their sentence, were only allowed to hold anything "in possession" that fitted into two volumetrically controlled boxes. On 20 December 1994 (more than two months after having left Cookham Wood) I had written the following to Myra: "Just heard on the news that Michael Howard won't resign in spite of a report, I forgot the name, with 64 security recommendations. One of the problems was the amount of personal belongings which made a proper room spin impossible. I miss sitting in your over-spilled room.")[4]

When I got home, I realised I had been given the wrong bag. It contained information regarding some high-profile prisoners. I decided to give the bag to Myra's solicitor to have it handed back to the prison. To my consternation he said I would probably get a visit from the police to investigate how I came to be in possession of this bag. Thankfully he managed to solve the problem for me; it required going to another solicitor who took down what had happened, and then to yet another solicitor to have an affidavit sworn.

There seems to be a growing popularity of internet auction sites with murder items. So-called signatures by Myra appear once in a while on these sites, even items of her clothing. Similarly, the house of Fred and Rosemary West at 25 Cromwell Street, had to be demolished because of all the people who had an unhealthy interest in it. They just entered the premises for some macabre trophy hunting (For example, patio slabs were taken from the garden). The Kray twins prison possessions have also been auctioned, fetching astronomical prices.[5]

Absolutely anything goes to keep the myth alive. Home Office, Prison Service and press, the three of them have colluded in this "Alice in Wonderland" world, tearing off the blindfold of the Statue of Justice. Leaving all reason, common sense, and most importantly, justice behind. Even Home Office officials acknowledged that Myra had become a political prisoner. Many people within the Prison Service could tell me of numerous cases where prisoners, whose offences were similar or worse to those of Myra, had been released without a murmur. Local Review Committees had recommended her release. But obviously, the famous tabloid polls appeared to have weighed more heavily for the Home Office than all the lengthy reports made by governors, psychiatrists, probation

---

4. After six prisoners escaped from Whitemoor high security prison, Sir John Woodcock was called in, by Michael Howard, to chair an inquiry. He made many recommendations regarding security, surveillance, observation, vetting of prison staff, and prisoners' property. The Opposition called for the Home Secretary to resign.
5. The London gangsters who controlled an East London crime empire and who were eventually convicted of murder and other serious crimes (including the murder of Jack "The Hat" McVitie) who served many years in prison and who each died still serving their life sentence. They became a kind of "prison royalty."

officers, chaplains, personal officers and psychologists who had known Myra for years and who the Home Office pays to write these reports. It seemed that the Home Office never took any positive action to counteract the barrage of fictitious and malicious articles;[6] many of which had negative consequences on Myra's life in prison. Original decisions made to make life for someone as unfortunately unique as Myra more tolerable were retracted out of fear of publicity.

There was a wide belief that Myra lived a holiday camp existence with numerous privileges, whereas the truth is that she was segregated to a vast extent from other prisoners for her protection and for the maintenance of good order and discipline (this was in her last year to 18 months at Cookham Wood Prison). She was often left with fewer privileges than were given to the most disruptive inmate serving a six-months sentence.

Not only did the Home Office not counteract the relentless flow of articles about Myra, whenever an article appeared their press office would be on the phone interrogating the Governor about it: "Is it true, has Myra been shopping in the shopping centre?" I was there when the press office phoned about this and heard the Governor reassure them that Myra had not been out shopping. I remember being surprised the Home Office would, in fact, take these stories seriously, and thereby, in a way, contribute to the media hype. About half a decade later the shopping story continued, this was when Myra had to be temporarily transferred back to Cookham Wood because of building repair works being carried out on the section at HM Prison Highpoint where she was housed; BBC commented: "Hindley … will return to Cookham Wood in Kent from where she had been taken out on shopping trips in the past." (BBC Teletext 1999)

A lot of pressure was put on consecutive Governments to keep Myra inside, as it was feared that the overriding public opinion about her could win or lose elections. I read that politician Harry Greenway had said that, although he thought that "Myra had paid her debts to society, she should not be released because this would lead to riots on the streets."

6. To give an example of the sheer relentless volume of print and other media devoted to Myra: In just one random year, 1994, roughly 150 (the definite number is doubtlessly higher) articles/ broadcasts were dedicated to Myra. Only a very small proportion of those are, in fact, sympathetic to her, and these precious few are totally neutralised by the welter of "media overkill."

As far as I am aware, this is the only Western European country where the anticipated behaviour of the people and public opinion can determine a prisoner's sentence and release. She had become a political headache of their making. The "policy" regarding Myra at head office appeared to veer between pretending she was not there and a succession of knee-jerk reactions. As Myra described them: "The Home Office and its public relations rag, *The Sun*."

The Home Office and Prison Service seemed to treat Myra like any other prisoner when it was convenient for *them* to do so, and to *her* disadvantage. By the same token they would treat *her* differently from any other prisoner when it was advantageous to *them*, but to Myra's detriment—even after her death the Home Office *still* continued to treat her differently—I think the only reason her confidential files have been released, at least 50 years early, is for no other reason than that she is Myra Hindley.

Even after she received her whole life tariff, no concessions were made regarding her regime. Every decision concerning Myra had to be approved, or more often vetoed, by Ministers. In December 1994, Myra received her whole life tariff. On 30 November she had written telling me:

> "I'm trying to analyse what I really feel about this impending tariff. I know I said I'm frightened, and I needed to tell you so that I didn't feel as frightened...I'd like to be braver or stronger and be able to say I'm not frightened, just apprehensive, but I can't say I'm not frightened because I am. I'm angry too, that [they] have dragged it out to the very end, resulting in questions in the House which will—is designed to—launch a media onslaught and ruin and make miserable yet another Christmas for my mother, Sharon and Bill...What I don't want...is any false sympathy or any real sympathy, from anyone in here. I don't want to see anyone—except you—or talk to anyone except anyone with anything constructive to offer...I want to be left alone, just as I do at Christmas."

She had the "natural life" sentence for almost five years before anyone bothered to inform her. When Myra was finally told about it, Prison Service head/area office gave the instruction to put her on suicide watch, even though there was no indication she was a suicide risk. Although it was meant to be for one night only, staff "misinterpreted" the instructions and continued their routine of switching on her cell light every half-hour which inevitably meant a range of sleepless nights. She was also put on a constant escort; this meant an officer accompanying her wherever she went during the day and then she was observed throughout the night. No reason was given for this instruction. The decision to put Myra on suicide watch was reported as medically indefensible and if she continued to be managed as a presumed suicide risk with special observation and other restrictions, her mental health and mental stability *would* be jeopardised.

Myra wrote to me on 27 January 1995 saying that when the visiting psychiatrist came to see her, he turned to one of the assisting governors and said:

> "Is she Category A [high risk]?"
> "No."
> "Category E [escape]?"
> "No," said the psychiatrist, "she is Category Hindley, uniquely treated to her detriment."

He then said to Myra: "Let me shake your hand. I've never seen anyone endure what you have with such patience and dignity."

A member of staff told Myra, who inquired about the insane restrictions put on her at the time, all he could do was to register his protest, which he had done. He explained to her it was all performance-related pay nowadays and whoever challenged anything or refused to do something, did not get paid.

The Prison Officers Association (POA) made Myra's life difficult by unnecessarily curtailing her privileges as an orderly; for example, they locked her in when they should have not. I had the impression the POA had singled her out to be used as a pawn on the chessboard of internal prison politics, this regardless of the fact that even head office (tariff unit) had urged delicate handling and support after Myra had been given the worst possible news any prisoner could receive: the fact that she was subject to a whole life tariff.

The POA also made an issue of her phone calls and visits. Myra, who was in the sick bay for both health and safety reasons, made her phone calls either from the sick bay with an officer present or the chaplains' office with of course a chaplain present. She offered to pay for the calls made. The fact that she made her calls from the chaplaincy was leaked to the press, so the press office phoned the prison to inquire; therefore, the prison felt obliged to stop this arrangement. Because I was the one she called (and this was mentioned in a *Sun* article) my then employer felt he "had to let me go."

The POA insisted Myra go down to the wing to make her phone calls; for safety reasons this took place in the evening when the other inmates were locked in. Sometimes she could not get to the phone because of some "incident" or shortage of staff. It also happened that, when she got to the phone, staff had "forgotten" to switch the phone on. Prison phone calls are taped, and ours were most probably also listened to, as they were the last of the day; although phone calls should only be randomly monitored. Because of the many leaks to the press from the prison, and with a "mole" still not unearthed, Myra sometimes chose not to use the phone when certain members of staff were on duty. Virtually any member of staff could listen to the recorded calls, interpret them in any way they wanted and (though breaking the law) make use of their content by passing or selling it to, for example, *The Sun*. We were told we could not use Dutch words for security reasons; I am pretty sure, though, that quite a few prison phone calls are held wholly in one foreign language or another. Apparently ex-MP Terry Dicks held the opinion that Myra should be banned from all contact with the outside world.

In spite of all this the way Myra was and continues to be perceived is illustrated in the following quote made ten years after her death: "She remained, however, a powerful and highly intelligent character who could bend the prison's organisation to her will" (Robert McCrum, *The Observer*, Sunday 28 October 2012).

Her regime was in stark contrast to that of IRA terrorists at the special unit at HM Prison Whitemoor. Michael Howard, then Home

Secretary, defended the luxury and said this was justified to compensate to some extent for the regime. Some of these compensations included free international telephone calls and the possibility to order lobster, steak or smoked salmon. The officers did the shopping. Home Office appeasement policy was to keep the terrorists happy and minimise their reasons for protest or riot. So they received nearly unsupervised visits, no rub-down searches and their visitors were not searched. Both Derek Lewis, the then Director General of the Prison Service, and Howard justified those conditions. In Myra's case, they knew she would not start a riot, so they could easily let themselves be dictated to by the tabloids and at the same time look tough. Even Myra's security category had on occasion been raised from B to A; this because of press intrusion and the subsequent furore it instigated; only to be later changed back again.

Just as Myra was kept in prison for political reasons, so were an army of Irish prisoners *released* for purely political reasons; this took place under the early release scheme that was part of the Good Friday Agreement. Patrick Magee was one of them. He was given eight life sentences in 1986 for the bombing of the Grand Hotel in Brighton where the Conservative Party Conference was being held, killing five people and maiming countless others. He served 13 years; his minimum tariff was 35 years.

Myra had this to say in a letter from Highpoint Prison on 17 November 1998:

> "Did you see *The Guardian* on the 11th, about the release of Martina Anderson and Ella O'Dwyer, two IRA women given 5 life sentences for the Hyde Park and other bombings in the 80s,? They were at Durham for a long time, before I got there, and were transferred to Northern Ireland, and released under the so-called Good Friday Peace agreement. Dozens of dedicated terrorists have been and are being released, supposedly in return for the decommissioning of weapons from both Loyalist and Republican groups, but as someone pointed out, so far, not even a single bullet has been handed in. And of course, we don't have political prisoners in Britain!"

Moving up north

> "I've concluded that as long as I'm in Cookham Wood I will be rooted in concrete, and my spirit stifled almost to extinction. Almost every week, sometimes every day, there is a battle of some kind to be fought, and I'm exhausted almost beyond my strength. I know that things will never change for the better, irrespective of individual goodwill. I've been here for so long I've become etched into the psyche of the prison and it into me, and it's not a healthy or desirable situation to be in. I feel like a problem that can't be solved or resolved. The same is true of my phone calls and visits."

At this point (she wrote the above on 13 February 1995) Myra asked to be transferred to Durham. It was not easy for her to make the decision to ask for this, it was a retrograde step. She had been in this prison 12 years earlier and her time there had psychologically and emotionally depleted her; in her mind it remained a "dark place."

She had enquired about other options, but there was no other alternative and staying at Cookham Wood had become untenable for various reasons. Firstly I could not visit her, this was refused for publicity reasons—although permission for our visits *was* finally approved at Ministerial level, but by this time Myra had already applied for a transfer—Moreover, there were the constant leaks to the press.

At first, after her move back to Durham, the prison seemed decent, and many of the staff *were* decent and helpful; but after a while problems started to emerge: interfering, difficulties at the gate, and so forth. There was certainly no "slipping in Durham jail" as one rag suggested I did. I had to brace myself for every visit just because of the hassle of getting into the prison. Furthermore, the meddling in the most basic and important of needs, that is, visits and phone calls was almost a repeat performance of the problems Myra had had at Cookham Wood, all amounting to the same thing: certain staff putting pressure on management by making complaints for whatever reason; leading to a clampdown out of fear of publicity.

Shortly after Myra was moved to Durham Prison, she fractured her femur in a fall, which meant a long spell on the prison hospital wing. Myra said in a letter to me of 24 April 1995:

> "I don't remember much at all about Monday, except for the horrendous pain of being transferred from the bed to the stretcher on the floor…and vultures with cameras while I was lying strapped in the stretcher with my dressing gown over my face as they carried me from the ambulance to the hospital. And the same thing in reverse when I left. They sent extra police who ringed the ambulance and [kept] the press at arm's length, and although I had two blankets covering my face with my arm across it, dozens of camera lights flashed through."

Myra's health was generally rather poor; she suffered, for example, from osteoporosis (the bane of long term, older female inmates) and angina. One of the various medications Myra took on a daily basis was the compound chloral hydrate, a sedative to help her sleep. She mentioned that during her years with Ian Brady she already suffered from sleeplessness and didn't sleep a lot, whereas, as she said, he slept like a log. When still at Cookham Wood I had tried to help her improve her health a little by, for example, bringing in some additional healthy food. In Durham this was not possible; although I did on the occasion sneak some wild garlic into the prison. In spite of having been repeatedly advised by (prison) doctors to stop smoking, she just could not give up the habit and continued to smoke heavily.

The Governor at Durham at the time assured her that she would never have to return to H-wing (the female wing there), mainly for safety reasons. But he left (he became area manager and remained to a certain degree involved in her case). His successor decided she *did* have to go back to the wing. Many of the staff thought this was a ludicrous idea as Myra could just about hobble around with a stick, and going back to the wing would be a risk to her. It was April 1996, and I was there visiting her when she was told she had to move back to H-wing. I had never seen her look so despairing.

One of the governors told Myra that her management was to a certain extent out of his hands and lay with the Lifer Management Unit at head office, but there I was told they could not do anything because it was seen as "operational" meaning it was a matter for the individual prison. No-one was prepared to make a constructive decision. So from then on Myra stayed most of the time in her cell on the wing. She was there with prisoners who had determinate sentences and other lifers who went on home leave.

Our visits in the visiting-room were something of an ordeal: either because of the other visitors staring at us out of curiosity, or when "alone" with prison officers when we had to pull our chairs forward so that we could be observed by them. The silence was intense. The sides of my fingernails turned black because of the stressful situation. Myra saw I was on the edge of a nervous breakdown and suggested we stop the visits.

There was little prospect the situation in Durham Prison would change. Myra on 20 November 1996:

> "...I've talked to him [one of the governors] before now about routinely monitored visits in that room 'at the back' and he told me with security being uber alles, the Governor wouldn't agree, and if I took my matter to Head Office, they wouldn't agree either. I pointed out that I'm not a security prisoner, and if *The Times* is to be believed, I should be in an open prison by now. But I'm not; I'm stuck on this poxy security wing, where we are all treated as security prisoners. I'll have to 'use' Yvonne, who gets periodic home leave, as 'ammunition', but I know what 'they' will say; that I can't be treated the same as her because she has whatever her tariff is, while I have a whole life one. To which I will respond by saying if I have to be treated differently from her, why can't I be treated differently to the rest of the wing population where my visits are concerned."

In Durham, it had been said and written that Myra spent too much of the last 30 years of her life in isolation for different reasons at different times. This is what she wrote to me:

"...I don't know what his [a doctor's] interpretation of 'too much' is. I spent 6 months on '43[7] at my own request, in the late '60s, when I and another inmate just couldn't handle the endless fights and all sorts of nasty things the women on the wing were doing to each other, and the doctor told me she had never seen me look so well and peaceful. I've spent several weeks here and there at Cookham's Healthcare, with chest infections; also after having been assaulted; and that year to 18 months I spent there before I moved was hardly isolation when the cells were regularly full of other inmates."

Myra wrote to me on 5 June 1996 in a letter about life in prison:

"...It's just like watching the same reel of film over all the years, over and over again. Nothing changes; the characters all playing their respective parts, and the vast majority of time I feel totally detached from it all. This is not because I consider myself to be any better or any worse than anyone else, it is the same conversations which rarely deviates from crime, past offences, drugs, etc. ad nauseam. An officer asked me last week if I didn't get fed up with being cooped up in here [her cell on H-wing in Durham]. I said I'd rather be cooped up in here than un-cooped out on the wing...but people can't understand why I choose to be alone. They may be able to if they took every day of all the years I've spent in prison and strung them all together like a chain but lost sight of each link as it receded into what feels like infinity."

And on June 7:

"I've just remembered something in my parole dossier, written from here [Durham], in 1980...that I was subtle and dangerous in the way I phrased questions (meaning I asked awkward, logical questions to which there was no logical reply to be found, only standard institutional parlance, woefully inadequate. e.g. '...for reasons of security which cannot be divulged': that was the answer given when I arrived here and asked why I couldn't have

7. Rule 43 allows prisoners to be segregated or isolated normally for their own protection (although now Prison Rule 45 it is still known quaintly and routinely by its former number).

my typewriter which I'd had for years in Holloway, and the same reply when I asked why I wasn't allowed to have a pumice stone, which I'd also had in Holloway. And the stock reply to petitions, which, when I was 'called up' by the Governor when the reply eventually came, usually after about 6 months...I used to recite in unison, 'The Secretary of State has fully considered your petition but is not prepared to grant your request'. Never any reason given, and it had been as near to the Secretary of State as Land's End is to John O'Groats). And it goes on to say that I'm at my most dangerous with the written word. That, as I'm sure I said to you when I first read it, was meant as an indictment, but it's the nicest compliment I ever expected from the prison system."

And October 10:

"I had a room search this morning, or I would have finished writing to you by now. I knew I was long overdue for one, and the two guys who did it were the ones who did my first one. They were really good, and put everything back where it was, and I sent a message down to them to ask that when they 'did' my bed, would they turn the mattress over for me because I can't do it myself—so they did. It didn't take them long, hardly any time at all; they know (were probably told) that I'm not into nasty old drugs or any illegal anythings. I know that some members of the DST[8] are, or can be bastards, and I really appreciated the way these two did my room, and although I wouldn't say 'thank you for searching my cell' I asked (the principal officer) to let them and whoever their boss is know how grateful I was at the professional way they did my cell-search. You'll probably think I'm stupid for doing that, but I'm sure you also know that I like to give credit where it's due."

◊

On *Question Time* (23 January 1997) Frank Dobson MP put forward another excuse why Myra should stay in prison. I paraphrase it: Myra

8. Dedicated search team.

should not be released "because this is a child-loving country, and it treasures its children." So, obviously, her continuous imprisonment had nothing to do with legal reasons! Also, the rank hypocrisy of this answer is clear, as the UK fares pretty badly compared to other developed countries regarding teenage pregnancies, child abuse, child neglect and child poverty.

In a report by UNICEF[9] in 2007 about children's general well-being, the UK came at the bottom of the list. England and Wales topped the league for the large number of incarcerated young adults (aged 18 to 20) with 8,514 behind bars, making up 11.4 per cent of total inmates (2006). More recently still, on 7 April 2016 Mark Easton, home affairs editor BBC noted that "Since 2004 more than 200 children have been given life sentences in England and Wales. Since 1990 in the rest of Europe it is two." Probably even more disturbing is the fact that Britain has the worst record in Europe for domestic child killings, and the fear is these figures will keep on rising (3 December 2013, *The Daily Telegraph*). If a country cares for its children it would not send women with children to prison for trivial offences, as this often means their children will have to be put into care.

Frank Dobson's comment about Myra Hindley has become even more ludicrous in light of the allegations of child abuse by members of the Establishment and the reluctance of the police to investigate—not to mention the despicable behaviour of councillors and the police in the child abuse cases such as Rotherham, Rochdale and so forth.

It is difficult to find figures regarding child abuse from other European countries that are comparable in a meaningful form. The National Society for the Prevention of Cruelty to Children is unambiguous about these figures, though: one in 10,000 children in this country is abused by a stranger, and one in eight is the victim of abuse by family, relatives or acquaintances. ChildLine supports this position: in 95 per cent of all calls made to them concerning sexual abuse, the abuser is related to, or known to, the child. Could it be because of unconscious guilt that Myra received the opprobrium she did?

9. See www.unicef.org.uk

Dobson also said: "The state of the prisoner's mind is not important. *The views of the public must be taken into consideration.*"

And there was no case like Myra's, where the Home Office was more concerned with the "public mood" than with justice. What hope do you have when for the department you are dependent on you are not relevant anymore as a human being, let alone as a prisoner, but only what you have come to represent? How the Home Office handled Myra Hindley's case is to its eternal discredit and shame. I cannot described it as anything else than incredible political cowardice, hiding behind popular emotions whipped up by the media.

Hypnosis and Other Distractions

"It is essential that justice be done, and it is equally vital that justice not be confused with revenge, for the two are wholly different."

Oscar Arias

"Restorative justice is not a replacement of retributive justice, but a complement. It seeks the rehabilitation of the wrongdoer and the repair of the victim's injury."

Lewis B Smedes

CHAPTER 9

Hypnosis and Other Distractions

The first time Myra offered to be hypnotised (to try and help locate the body of Keith Bennett) was in 1987 and she had repeated this request periodically since then. She waited eight years for permission, and when her request was finally granted, it seemed as if Prison Service head office was doing all it could with its repressive regime to make it impossible for her to be psychologically strong enough to undergo hypnosis successfully.

Furthermore, her last application for hypnosis included an agreement by all parties that anything she said which was not connected or relevant to the enquiry would be erased from the tape. This time the police decided that they wanted the whole video, in its entirety, and also wanted it kept by them. Naturally, Myra had concerns about this reversal of the agreement because of the possibility of misuse. She told me that John Stalker (former Deputy Chief Constable of Greater Manchester Police) apparently once said that there were more leaks in the Manchester Crime Investigation Department than in a sieve. And Myra told me she *knew* it was the police who first leaked her confessions to the press, and then leaked the plans for hypnosis. She, also, only ever thought of a cassette-tape recording, not a video; as she wondered if it would be used just for what it was intended—another search on the moors. Especially since, as she told me, several of those awful photographs of one of the victims were appropriated years after the trial and were being used in a police training school and even in the *Police Gazette*. What's more, they wanted to stipulate that even the preliminary meetings were to be videoed. These were meetings between the hypnotist and Myra so that they could get to know each other and Myra could relax with her.

She was utterly committed to hypnosis, but some people suggested she just used it as a bargaining tool (Myra the manipulator) in order to be allowed to receive visits from me; yet all she wanted was confirmation that when she made the retrograde step to go back to Durham, the Prison Service would not backtrack on its promise by saying I was not allowed to visit her. I found this request of hers reasonable and prudent. After all, the authorities had been chipping away at her privileges for months. (One of the governors said they were "twitching" at head office). She also felt that, apart from the transfer out of Cookham Wood, my visits would give her the support she needed, and thus make the whole situation conducive to hypnosis. In one of Ian Brady's rants, he said that he believed that Myra would fake a hypnotic trance, just to try for parole. Myra:

> "And Brady has started again—he's terrified they'll find Keith Bennett because it will deprive him of his last hold over people. He just wants this saga to continue."

In the end she did not undergo hypnosis, as by that time, after her move to Durham, her health had deteriorated too much.

◊

The "Myra industry"

There is yet another reason this Myra industry could continue as it did, and still does to an extent: quite a few people quickly learnt that there was money to be made from her. Apart from the obvious suspects, the newspapers and journalists, many people around her also made a quick or easy profit from her: it was alleged that there were various "moles" in the prison and Prison Service, prisoners, ex-prisoners, "sympathisers," "friends", and so on who passed on information to journalists and others. The media also enticed some of the families of the victims in a way I found distasteful.

Few people would argue that there is anything more devastating in life than losing one's child, especially in such an horrendous manner; I would, however, question the way the press exploited the grief of these families. Financially, it no doubt has helped them, some of the families had armed themselves with agents, and apparently demanded money for any reaction, statement or even just a few words, but in many other ways it must have been to their detriment, as it appeared to have kept them frozen in time and in a perpetual state of bitterness, torment, and vengeance. Do words exist for such cynicism on the part of our gutter press?

The notable exception to the above was Alan Bennett, brother of Keith Bennett, who after corresponding with Myra for some time regarding the location of his brother's grave, visited her in prison to discuss this issue further with her. She wrote to me about it and described it as quite an incredible visit. She mentioned that he told her that he never could and never would be able to associate her with the person she was when with Brady and while, of course, his main concern was Keith, he had no "bad" feelings towards her.

A problem with victim involvement: A personal view

Involving victims of crimes in sentencing or as promised by Jack Straw when Home Secretary "to put the victim at the heart of the justice system" is turning the justice system on its head. In effect, the logical conclusion from this would be that the length of a sentence could then depend on how forgiving the victim was. The views of the victim on how a criminal act has affected him or her emotionally and psychologically can only corrode the essence of the justice system, its neutrality and objectivity. For is not allowing emotive involvement, in fact, negating the whole point of *why* we have a justice system? "Justice normally disregards the feelings of the aggrieved; that is actually what it is for." (*The Times*, 9 December 1994)

Victims' rights are not in opposition to the rights of offenders and should not be portrayed as such. Seeking justice and humane treatment for offenders is not in any way denying or underestimating the concerns or grief of victims, and should not be presented as such. We do not have to take sides. For example, when new evidence was unearthed proving that the men convicted of murder in "the Carl Bridgewater" case[1] were innocent, the *Daily Express* front page headline on 11 April 1996 was: "Why don't they think of Carl?" As if acquitting the innocent men, who had wrongfully spent 18 years in prison, was somehow a betrayal of the victim.

◊

In one case in America I heard of, two teenagers were found guilty of murdering the owner of a firearms store. In court, his widow produced a huge photo of her husband saying, "[T]his is what he looked like when he left for work that morning." She then held up a box containing his ashes and said, "[T]his is what he looked like when he came back that evening." Powerful stuff, everyone in court agreed, and it swayed the sentence for the two teenagers from life with parole to life without parole. This kind of performance is better placed in the theatre than in the courtroom.

Similarly in the case of Charles Manson and his "Family"; the relatives of film actress Sharon Tate (one of the Manson Family's brutally murdered victims) were influential in changes to the parole system, that is, allowing relatives of victims to make victim impact statements in court during sentencing and having the last word at the Parole Board. The result of this was the repeated blocking of the release of three women of the Manson Family. These women were, and the surviving two are, consistently recommended for parole by prison review boards but, despite the indisputable evidence of their reform and rehabilitation, the presence of the victims' relatives at the Parole Board has made the possibility of release remote. Patricia (sister of Sharon) Tate's position was clear-cut: Patricia Krenwinkel's (one of the Manson Family) expressions of remorse were lies, she hadn't changed a bit in 25 years. According to Patricia Tate:

1. The four men who were found guilty of killing 13-year-old Carl Bridgewater in 1978 had, after nearly two decades of imprisonment, their convictions overturned.

> "I don't care if she has rehabilitated. I don't care anything about her except for that she should stay in prison for the rest of her living life."

Her counsel dismissed Krenwinkel's petition as "crocodile tears."

It was said about Susan Atkins, who was denied parole 13 times before her death in 2009 of brain cancer at the age of 61:

> "...because Susan Atkins showed no mercy to her victims, we, therefore, are duty-bound to follow her inhumanity and show no mercy to *her*."

And more recently: in July 2016, Leslie van Houten (aged 66), the youngest of the Manson followers was denied parole again; she has applied for parole 20 times before. She has now been in prison for over 40 years and is regarded a model prisoner. With a petition, signed by 140,000 people, the relatives of the victims opposed her release.

Justice versus revenge

In my view, this "eye-for-an-eye" approach has nothing to do with justice, but everything to do with revenge. Proportionality should be the watchword in relation to both the rights of victims and the punishment of offenders, not a return in the direction of the long discredited or nowadays largely Eastern notion of, metaphorically speaking, "blood money." Victims of crime should receive all the support they feel they need to help them cope with their rage and pain. Victim services and restitution are vitally important and necessary, and there is still scope for improvement in this area. The worrying trend, however, is that victim's rights are too often becoming synonymous with vengeance (some victim support groups are apparently funded by the tabloid press, at least according to Anne McArthur who I mention in the dedication at the start of this book). A just system of law balances and protects both sets of interest.

Even for a criminologist it is sometimes tempting to lose objectivity when confronted with a crime. My Professor of Criminology at the University of Amsterdam once mentioned an incident where he got mugged and robbed of his bag. He jokingly said it was very fortunate that nobody in the week or so after the event asked his opinion on anything relating to crime and punishment.

In sharp contrast to the above, I want to mention here a most moving, impressive and humbling account by Marian Partington. Her article in *The Guardian*(1996), "Salvaging the Sacred" and her book *If You Sit Very Still* (2012) describe her long, difficult and painful journey through agonising grief, and ultimately to forgiveness after her sister Lucy was abducted and murdered by Fred and Rosemary West. Marian finally wrote to Rose West a letter of forgiveness and even compassion. She tells that it had taken her ten years to write this letter and another four years to post it as she first wanted to come to the point that she did not need or expect a reply. The reply Marian got was from the prison, who relayed her the message that Rosemary West did not wish to receive any more letters from her.

◊

An extended example of Myra's writing

Myra wrote the following in Holloway sometime between 1974 and 1976. It begins with words from Tolstoy's *Diary of a Madman*. The part about the clock-face of time (or life) was something she remembered from and was based around one of D H Lawrence's books — *Women in Love.*

> "What is life for? To die? To kill myself at once? No, I'm afraid. To wait for death till it comes? I fear that even more. Then I must live. But what for? In order to die? And I cannot escape from that circle. I pick up a book, read, and forget myself for a moment, but then again, the same question, the same horror. I lie down and close my eyes. It's worse still.
>
> The thought of the mechanical succession of day following day, day following day, ad infinitum is one of the things that make my heart palpitate with real approach of madness. The terrible bondage of this tick-tock

of time, this twitching of the hands of the clock, this eternal repetition of hours and days; oh God, it's too awful to contemplate. And there is no escape from it; no escape.

I lie here alone, confronted by the terrible clock with its eternal tick-tock. All life, all life resolved into this: tick-tock, tick-tock, tick-tock, then the striking of the hour; then the tick-tock, tick-tock, tick-tock and the twitching of the clock fingers.

I've wondered if I'd be very surprised on rising each morning, to realise my hair had turned white. I have felt it turn white so often under the intolerable burden of my thoughts and of my sensations. Yet it remains as brown as ever, perhaps because I'm healthy though run-down. Perhaps it is only my unabateable health which leaves me so exposed to the truth. If I were sickly, I would have illusions and imaginations. As it is, there is no escape. I can never escape from my thoughts. I am placed immovably before the clock-face of life. In vain I try to read, to study. But I'm not really reading or studying; I'm watching the fingers twitch across the eternal, mechanical, monotonous clock-face of time. I don't really live; I merely watch. I feel like a little twelve-hour clock vis-a-vis with the enormous clock of eternity

But time stands still, immutable.

I've never longed for death before (I don't now; I just want to cease to exist.); not ever, not even in those worst moments of my past life, in spite of everything that has happened. In all the years in prison, facing an unknown, obscure and even doubtful future, I've never wished to die, as deadly as life has often seemed. I've preferred life, mere existence even, to death, just like the Dostoevskian character who meditated thus: 'I would live on a high rock, on such a narrow ledge that I'd only have room enough to stand; and the ocean, everlasting darkness, everlasting solitude, everlasting tempest raging around me. If I had to remain standing on a square yard of space, all my life, a thousand years, eternity-it would be better to live so, than to die at once.'

This is how I used to feel; that I would prefer any kind of life to death—for death, in my agnostic years, was so final. But then I found a reason to live, to really live, and not just for sake of merely being alive, as before. God gave me back my faith, something I had lost so easily before because it was my childhood faith and was weak, like a feeble child.

At the age of eighteen I met a man who within months convinced me that there was no God at all. He could have told me that the earth was flat, that the sun rose in the west, that the moon was made of green cheese, and I would have believed him, such were his powers of persuasion, his lofty, convincing manner of speech which fascinated me because he spoke in an esoteric tongue which I could never fully comprehend, could only grasp at the odd sentence here and there and believed it to be the gospel truth.

He convinced me that my faith, that all religions, were superstitions instilled in us as a conventional norm. Religion, he said, was just a crutch to hobble through life on; the opium of the people, he said, as Marx had. And I believed him because I thought I loved him, and his arguments were so convincing he demolished my tiny precepts with a single sentence. So he became my god, my idol of worship, and I worshipped him blindly, more blindly than the congenitally blind, for many long years ... Then the old, old scales fell from my eyes, from my mind's eye, and I could see, really see, for the first time in too many years. I could think my own thoughts in freedom, instead of those of the god who had indoctrinated his spellbound disciple. For the spell had always held me as long as I could never penetrate the veil with which he clothed himself and which enveloped him in his own mysterious self, with his own brand of 'theology'. And with the scales fallen from my eyes, I looked at him, my god, my idol. I looked up at him, for he'd always been far above me, aloof and out of reach. But now I could reach up and touch him, and did so, and he crashed from the pedestal I'd built for him. Like Flaubert's Madame Bovary, I touched my idol, and the gilt rubbed off onto my fingers: dust and ashes of a dead love flaked around my feet and I stepped out from amongst the debris, shook the last remaining speck from my whole self and walked away at last, freed from the irons and fetters which had bound me for so long.

I floated for a long time on a spiritual high, and on a new-found freedom from the bondage I'd been in for so long. But then that dreaded dark night of the soul descended on me and covered me in a deep black cloak that left me in darkness. And this time, it was the intolerable burden of the guilt I carried inside me that weighed me down. My heart feels broken, crushed and torn, bleeding and aching, and my soul is heavy and weeps without ceasing. My mind, like that clock, ticks on relentlessly, thoughts swirling uncontrollably, and there is no peace, no rest…I am so afraid. I feel bereft of hope, my equilibrium shattered, my will hanging together by a single, flimsy weak thread. I'm frightened. I'm hurtling downwards into the pit of black despair, and I struggle frantically to stop myself. I grab frenziedly at anything to try to break the fall. Occasionally I find a foothold or something to grasp hold of and I cling, trembling with relief to the frail ledge. But suddenly it crumbles and I begin to plunge downwards again. I feel like giving up the struggle, allowing myself to slither to the bottom where I can at least lie and let the exhaustion seep out of me, and some kind of peace imbue my tired body. But there would be no peace of mind; my thoughts would still clamour cacophonously within my brain, and my heart would continue to ache, to break. So I keep up the struggle not to go down, and if I must go down, I'll go down fighting not to."

◊

The following are further excerpts from Myra's letters to me, the first on 7 July 1998:

"Did you see or hear about Brady's escape plot that was planned? It was in the Sunday Express a couple of weeks ago. Thank God someone blew the whistle on him; he said he was going abroad, but I know he had some unfinished business to see to before he left. If I weren't in here, I'd be the first to go, and David Smith [Myra's brother-in-law][2] the second, to name but two of us. The Express got access to his personal computer where he'd typed in

2. Smith was key witness for the prosecution during the Moors Murders trial. He had entered into a financial arrangement with the *News of the World*, where the conviction of Brady and Hindley would benefit him greatly. The newspaper narrowly escaped contempt charges.

his plans, and a handwritten list—he hasn't changed a bit; still the same methodical planner of every contingency in case something went wrong. They also saw more than 200 powerful painkillers, which he'd hidden in various glasses (shades) cases; they weren't for euthanasia reasons; they were to be used if his plans failed. Now the idiot is on a 24 hr. suicide watch. I felt like writing to him and telling him to ask to go back to prison where it's so easy to commit suicide."

Sixteenth August 1998:

"...for two interesting things to note are that a 46 year old trained psychiatric nurse with tons of experience, said she thought he was fantasysing when he talked in round about ways about freedom, just as I thought, aged 19, when he was talking to me about his 'perfect murder', only she managed to get out when she realised that he was deadly serious, and she talked about the kind of person he was; good company sometimes, but volatile, angry and aggressive when she disagreed with him about anything."

Fourth December 1998:

"...You made me smile when you asked, in the postcard with the '60s tapes, if I was reliving my youth, for when I played the tapes, it was just as if I was. Quite a few of the tracks were made before I came to prison, and the rest of them when I was on the first offenders' wing, and later on E wing. And in those days I was happy, because I've told you I was relieved to come to prison because that awful life we lived was over, he needed me, rather than the other way round, and I met lots of really nice people. I've sometimes wondered if it was sad or pathetic to feel the way I did, but it was neither, it was simply true. I didn't *like* prison, but I didn't like much of life outside either."

I'd Like to Help You, But . . .

"May God have mercy on you, Myra Hindley, for ungodly men will have none."

Germaine Greer

CHAPTER 10

I'd Like to Help You, But...

Myra loved the book *A Man* by Oriana Fallaci. A phrase she once quoted in one of her letters to me and which she felt also applied to her was, "I'd love to help you but"... this is a fragment of a sentence from the book where people used to say to the main character, "I'd love to help you but... I've got a family, responsibilities, other things to consider and so forth." There was always a reason not to help; probably it was more a question of being too afraid. And I hope that the deafening silence around Myra's case from the various liberal-minded justice and human rights groups and also women's groups stemmed indeed from fear to speak out rather than wholesale tacit approval of how her case was dealt with and of her treatment.

But, fortunately, there was also an immeasurable amount of support, not just for Myra, but for myself as well: for example, when the press door-stepped me, the people who I shared the house with were wonderful and supportive. Also, when my somewhat revised article appeared in *The Independent on Sunday*, the newsagent was kind to me, and the green-grocer gave me some extra apples.

Myra received a lot of supportive letters. There were also people who wanted her autograph, pupils and students asking her for a contribution to some project or another, questionnaires, magazines asking for an article or an interview. And when Myra *did* give an interview (*Sunday Times*, 18 December 1994), she got swiftly punished for "embarrassing the Minister." It meant an immediate "crackdown" regarding her visits, also her solicitor's visits, and an investigation into how this could have happened. Meanwhile there was yet another "leak" to the *Sun* of confidential information from the Home Office regarding Myra. Most of these leaks remained, however, uninvestigated. She said to me once that it was quite a relief that many people who wrote to her did not give an address, because it was impossible to reply to everyone. Especially considering the time it took to fight all the battles within the Prison Service.

There were lots of well-wishers and people who had started a petition for her release; perhaps, surprisingly, she received very few nasty letters; for every nasty one she got, she received ten positive ones. Myra to me:

> "Almost every letter I've received—and they're still coming in—points out, at last, that my imprisonment has nothing to do with the crimes but solely with publicity and the politics of fear...More mail this morning: one woman from Warrington—where Risley is, up North[1]—said it's grossly unfair treatment and why should I spend the rest of my life in prison for the sake, not of justice, but what seems to be the Government's assessment of public opinion. And another from Bedfordshire said '[I]t seems that you are now the victim rather than the criminal'...Some of the letters I've had express sympathy and empathy and the writer's own sense of outrage about the political decision, fuelled by the tabloids to those tabloid-mentality members of the public, and have said '[A]s a feminist I'm doubly incensed that you're being doubly punished because you're a woman.'"

◊

One day Myra and I talked about a nature programme we had both seen and I asked her if watching that kind of programme did not make her feel even more incarcerated. She told me on the contrary that she derived great pleasure from watching them. She talked more about it in a next letter to me of 3 July 1996:

> "For years, the lifers room on North wing [at Cookham Wood] had only a black and white TV, and when I had to go in there to fill my flasks and wait for the kettle to boil, if a wildlife programme was on, I always wished I could see it in colour. I love to see the greenery, the flowers, the trees, birds

1. Risley Prison/Remand Centre.

and butterflies—everything of a 'rural' nature. That's why I loved to go out 'watering' in the summer evenings, being surrounded by flowers everywhere (and the trees) and actually hearing the dry soil and half-wilting flowers drinking in the water. I used to use the hosepipe to give all the flowerbeds a thorough soaking, and the watering can for the hanging baskets—the scent of flowers was exquisite as the water soaked them as well as the soil... And what I meant when I said I always wondered over all the years if the sea was still blue was in a metaphorical sense—was the sea still blue; were horses, sheep and cows still in the fields, meadows and paddocks; were there still haystacks, was harvest time still harvest time. I could go on and on, but I won't."

My mind goes back to the time at Cookham Wood: when possible we would go to the gym during lunch break to play tennis, as part of Myra's medical regime. Instead of going through the prison we walked across the prison grounds to the gym. One day the fence was being repaired. This fence normally has wooden planks about half way up, to prevent people from looking in or out. Because of the repairs, part of the wood was taken down, so it was possible to see beyond the fence. Myra said that, for once, she preferred to sit outside the gym; and, for the next half-hour, she just sat gazing at the trees and the bit of green that was visible.

July 1998:

"Nien, I've come a long way in the past few months. I've thought positive, acted positively and constructively, and am slowly moving in the direction I should have begun moving in donkey's years ago. I make all my own decisions; lay down my own rules, and I feel strong and fighting fit. I *know* I'll get to see [name of the psychoanalyst] eventually; I've resolved that I will, and now I've got going, there's no stopping me. I've got my life together, and am happy with it—though I do wish you'd sodding visit me some time; I miss you and want to spend a couple of hours talking with you. So—and I'm not bullying you—start getting your act together, because you know as well as I do that one small step leads to giant strides, and you can do anything you want if your heart is in. Like you, I'd rather do nothing at all; just sit and read, do my library work, for I need the wages, watch T/V, write

> my letters, make my phone calls and have my visits, and sleep away the rest of the time. As you know, I've done that too, I've been there, and I'm definitely not going back there. I know it's harder to achieve what you want on the outside, but if it were me out there, I'd think of it as a challenge and take it on straight away—like this weed-filled, nettle-type-triffids filled garden."[2]

Like all other legally sane people convicted of murder after 1965, Myra Hindley had a right to expect parole in due course of time. Yet so ingrained was the feeling of public opinion generated against her that it infected every level of our society. It dictated the terms on which the allegedly neutral Parole Board made some of its recommendations, and in which members of the allegedly neutral Prison Service had behaved, and last but not least how a succession of allegedly neutral Home Secretaries had pronounced judgement.

On the 25th November 2002, it was declared by the Law Lords *that judges, not the Home Secretary,* would from now on decide the length of tariffs (David Blunkett, Home Secretary 2001–2004, it is believed, knowing he was going to lose this case, "in a panic" indicated to Greater Manchester Police that they could perhaps find new charges against Myra).

This ruling of the Law Lords would have meant her possible release. Myra had conveniently died ten days earlier .... she has been a casualty of this shameful episode in judicial history and so has the truth, of course. But the casualty we may live to regret is the one that we have so nonchalantly allowed to be hi-jacked by our careless and conscienceless media, in Myra Hindley's name: and that is "justice."

Lesley McLaughlin:

> "Myra Hindley, the person, has been appropriated by the media and the people and transformed into Myra Hindley the symbol. Whatever she really was and is, is forever lost under the crushing weight of what she has come to represent. She has been engulfed, transmuted and regurgitated in

2. A small garden at Highpoint Prison that Myra looked after.

> the form of a mythical beast which bears little or no resemblance to the reality. This process of transmogrification—from human to monster—has been devastating in its ferocity and efficacy." (*Media Representations of Myra Hindley*, p.47)

I have tried to rectify this image a little by giving a glimpse of the "real" Myra Hindley, the woman I knew; and thereby hopefully sowing a seed which at some point might help to lead to a reappraisal of Myra. After decades of "monstering," the task to rehabilitate her reputation is, of course, monumental. What happened to her should act as a warning to all of us of what can occur when we surrender the concept of justice, the rule of law, or even just human decency by descending into a modern-day witch-hunt.

When writing this, 20 years after I first met her, all the memories came flooding back. But I also felt guilt, guilt and regret that I did not come over immediately when she phoned, asking me to come and visit her because she was not feeling well. Next thing I knew I was hearing on the radio that she had died. Myra once said to me that she was afraid that she had become my Achilles heel; I assured her she could not be further from the truth.

These years will always remain one of the most important and instructive episodes in my life, and I feel privileged to have known her.

The Prisoner

STILL let my tyrants know, I am not doom'd to wear
Year after year in gloom and desolate despair;
A messenger of Hope comes every night to me,
And offers for short life, eternal liberty.

He comes with Western winds, with evening's wandering airs,
With that clear dusk of heaven that brings the thickest stars:
Winds take a pensive tone, and stars a tender fire,
And visions rise, and change, that kill me with desire.

Desire for nothing known in my maturer years,
When Joy grew mad with awe, at counting future tears:
When, if my spirit's sky was full of flashes warm,
I knew not whence they came, from sun or thunder-storm.

But first, a hush of peace—a soundless calm descends;
The struggle of distress and fierce impatience ends.
Mute music soothes my breast—unutter'd harmony
That I could never dream, till Earth was lost to me.

Then dawns the Invisible; the Unseen its truth reveals;
My outward sense is gone, my inward essence feels;
Its wings are almost free—its home, its harbour found,
Measuring the gulf, it stoops, and dares the final bound.

O dreadful is the check—intense the agony—
When the ear begins to hear, and the eye begins to see;
When the pulse begins to throb—the brain to think again—
The soul to feel the flesh, and the flesh to feel the chain.

Yet I would lose no sting, would wish no torture less;
The more that anguish racks, the earlier it will bless;
And robed in fires of hell, or bright with heavenly shine,
If it but herald Death, the vision is divine.

Emily Bronte

Select Bibliography

Birch, Helen (1993), *Moving Targets*, London: Virago

Boyle, Jimmy (1985), *Pain of Confinement*, London: Pan

Chippindale, Peter and Horrie, Chris (1990), *Stick It Up Your Punter, the Rise and Fall of The Sun*, London: Heineman

Cyriax, Oliver (1996), *The Encyclopedia of Crime,* London: Penguin

Jones, Janie (1993), *The Devil and Miss Jones,* London: Smith Gryphon Publishers

Kennedy, Helena (1993), *Eve Was Framed,* London: Vintage edition

Kirsta, Alix (1994), *Deadlier than the Male*, Glasgow: Harper Collins

Kozubska, Joanna (2014), *Cries for Help: Women Without a Voice, Women's Prisons in the 1970s, Myra Hindley and her Contemporaries*, Sherfield-on-Loddon: Waterside Press

McLaughlin, Lesley (2007), *Media Representations of Myra Hindley*, Lulu Publishing

Mitchell, David (1995), *Bluff Your Way into Law,* West Sussex: Ravette Publishing

Padel, Una and Stevenson, Prue (1988), *Insiders: Women's Experience of Prison,* London: Virago

Partington, Marian (2012), *If You Sit Very Still,* Bristol: Vala Publishing

Rusche, Georg and Kirchheimer, Otto (1939) *Punishment and Social Structure*, New Jersey: Transaction Publishers

Index

L

M

N

Q

R

S

T

U

V

W

Holloway Prison: An Inside Story
by Hilary Beauchamp
With a Foreword by Maggi Hambling

A compelling, true life account of her time working in this famous north-London prison. Hilary Beauchamp 'lifts the lid' on life inside, making the book a must for students of women's imprisonment or prison education. A unique and telling insight into life in a claustrophobic and sometimes violent atmosphere. An ideal primer on women's issues within the penal system. With eight colour pages of original artwork.

An excellent text… Hilary Beauchamp writes wonderfully, vividly and honestly'
Ben Whittaker, former barrister, MP and Government Minister

I have enormous admiration for Hilary Beauchamp and this book is a fascinating contribution in a field which has not been widely covered… She has a longstanding track record of quality projects… someone of total integrity'
Lord David Puttnam, film director

Paperback & ebook | ISBN 978-1-909976-23-8 | 2015 | 320 pages

Lightning Source UK Ltd.
Milton Keynes UK
UKHW020640210221
379137UK00004B/252